Runaway
Girl

CASEY WATSON

A beautiful girl. Trafficked for sex.
Is there nowhere to hide?

This book is a work of non-fiction based on the author's experiences.
In order to protect privacy, names, identifying characteristics,
dialogue and details have been changed or reconstructed.

HarperElement
An imprint of HarperCollins*Publishers*
1 London Bridge Street
London SE1 9GF

www.harpercollins.co.uk

First published by HarperElement 2016

17 18 19 20 LSC/C 10 9 8 7 6 5 4 3 2 1

A catalogue record of this book is
available from the British Library

PB ISBN 978-0-00-824423-1
EB ISBN 978-0-00-814259-9

Printed and bound in the United States of America by
LSC Communications

Find out more about HarperCollins and the environment at
www.harpercollins.co.uk/green

I'd like to dedicate this book to all those working in the care system in one form or another, for their dedication, hard work, and constant pushing for change and improved services for our young people. Despite budget cuts, government changes and constantly having to adapt to an increasing workload, you still strive for that light at the end of the tunnel. As a result, someone else in the care system will thrive, someone else will have a fair shot at a good life. I feel so proud to be able to be part of this, and if you, the reader, are thinking about joining the ranks of social care in some form, just go ahead and do it. The rewards far outweigh the difficulties we face.

Acknowledgements

As always, I'd like to thank my wonderful, dedicated team at HarperCollins. They have championed me from the start and continue to do so despite difficult times. My very patient agent, Andrew Lownie, deserves a medal for what he does, and it goes without saying how much I appreciate all he has done and continues to do. Thank you so much, Andrew. And as always, special thanks to my wonderful friend and mentor, Lynne. You know what an inspiration you are!

Preface

Around 3,000 children arrive in the UK alone every year seeking asylum, and unfortunately an estimated 5,000 young people – almost all of them girls – have been trafficked here since the late nineties. Our government then struggles to navigate 'complex and adult systems' (i.e. those designed for adults, as no one imagined children would migrate alone) to get them the support they need. They are sometimes known as 'hidden children'.

Chapter 1

January

There is a grandparenting moment – and it's one of the best ones – when, after a great deal of patience and fortitude, not to mention finger-crossing, you realise that you have *finally* got the baby off to sleep. And, though you love them (and with an intensity that can take your breath away), you are mighty glad that you can do the proverbial, and give them back to your offspring again.

It was into one such moment that my mobile exploded into life. My mobile that I'd forgotten I still had on me.

'Bloody hell, Case!' hissed Mike as I scrabbled to try to silence it. Which was a case of frantically slapping both hands over the offending cardigan pocket to muffle it, and beating a hasty retreat, backwards, from Dee Dee's bedroom.

And by some miracle, despite the shocking cacophony, she didn't stir. I missed the call, though, having clattered down the stairs before attempting to answer it, and gone

1

back into the living room. *And* shut the door, for good measure.

I finally pulled the phone out, long after it had ceased warbling at me, while Mike relocated the baby monitor to the coffee table, glaring at it as if willing it to remain silent. It had been a long, fraught hour getting the baby off, to be fair.

'Oh,' I said, 'it's John. As in Fulshaw. Wonder what he wants.'

Mike flumped down on the sofa beside me. 'Well, if it's "Would you mind taking in another ten-month-old baby?", that'll be a no.'

'Oh, hush,' I said. 'Go and make some coffee and stop moaning. She's down now, and she'll stay down. You know what she's like.'

'I'm not surprised,' said Mike, with feeling. 'What is it about flipping babies? I've never really got that. When you're tired you go to sleep. Problem solved. Easy. Why do they have to make it so *difficult*?'

I grinned at him, already pressing the return-call button on my mobile. As a veteran of two kids, four grandkids, and the various little ones we'd fostered, he knew that was one of the great unanswered questions precisely because there would never *be* an answer to it. An overtired baby was a simple but complicated beast; she *was* overtired, but the reasons could be myriad, from colic, to teething, to being too hot, cold or stimulated – it could even be the smell of my new perfume. But we'd got there and could relax now … well, after a fashion. And possibly not for long, given the call.

'Hi there, John,' I said moments later. 'So. To what do we owe the pleasure?'

'Oh, dear,' he said. 'I'm sorry to be calling you so late.'

'It's only eight, John. It's fine,' I reassured him. Though, while doing so, I was already taking stock of why he'd be calling. It was outside of office hours, so nothing routine or training-related, clearly. Which presumably meant a child he wanted us to take in.

Mike had picked up our coffee mugs but still lingered in the living room, obviously thinking the same thing.

'We've got a teenager on the way,' John explained, and I mouthed the word to Mike, who nodded. 'Coming to us via a rather circuitous route. Not from round here – well, to be precise, not from anywhere remotely round here. She's a Polish girl, apparently – not been long in the country, and all out of options.'

'What's happened to her?' I asked John as Mike headed to the kitchen.

'We're not entirely clear yet. She doesn't speak a lot of English and the details are sketchy. *Very* sketchy. So, to be truthful, I have no idea what we're dealing with yet.'

John not having any idea what we'd be dealing with was the case more often than not, so this, in itself, didn't faze me. Nor did what he *did* know – that she was 14, and had turned up at a social services building earlier, very distraught, in Hull, some 100 miles away. And, with no room at the inn via the local out-of-hours service, the 'problem' had eventually made its way to our fostering agency, and, as John was the supervising social worker and manager of our local office, to us.

'I'm expecting her within the hour,' he explained. 'Are you and Mike able to take her in? More to the point, are you even around? I did try the house phone.'

I explained that we were round at my son Kieron's house, babysitting his and his partner Lauren's baby daughter. 'But that's no big stress,' I added. 'They've only gone to the cinema. They'll be back in less than that, and then we can shoot home.'

'I'd be enormously grateful,' John said, and he sounded it. 'As I say, I've no idea what the deal is. The girl's apparently quite distressed, says she has nowhere to go, and has obviously been sleeping rough for a while. But I'm told she's otherwise healthy and seemingly sane; says she's not been harmed in any way.'

'D'you know any more than that?' I asked him, already forming a mental picture. *Otherwise healthy and seemingly sane.* I wondered what it must be like to be a 14-year-old girl all alone in a big, scary city.

'Not really. Only assumptions. You know what it's like. She says she has no parents, and nowhere to go back to, but that's probably questionable. We've seen it before, to be honest; parents sending their kids over here when they can't support them, with little more than a note with their name and age. And the kids are usually savvy enough not to give any details. But we shall see, eh?'

Indeed we would, I said, feeling the usual first stirrings of intrigue. 'So, what's her name?' I asked him.

'Adrianna. Or so she said. Anyway, thanks for stepping in, Casey. Doubt you'll have to have her long.'

I smiled at that as I disconnected. Or so *he* said.

The previous year had been a rather different one for us. We still had Tyler, of course, who we'd taken on permanently, and who was now a lanky 14-year-old. And he was so much a part of the family now, the 'foster' part of 'foster son' no longer even passed our lips. But after several intense years of fostering – and some harrowing experiences – we'd stepped temporarily off the hamster wheel as far as new long-term placements were concerned, and, having seen our last long-term foster child into her new forever home the previous March (a little girl with foetal alcohol syndrome called Flip), we'd begun a short fostering break.

Mostly, this was to support our son, Kieron. With him and Lauren's first baby, Dee Dee, coming along shortly after Flip left us (she who was currently not troubling the baby monitor, thankfully), we'd decided to focus on helping them as much as possible, as we had no way of knowing how well Kieron would cope with the upheaval in his life. Kieron had Asperger's syndrome, which was a mild form of autism, and though we were confident that, between them, he and Lauren would manage as well as any other fledgling parents, there was always this thought in the back of my mind that a safety net would be no bad thing at all.

So, since Flip had gone, we'd only agreed to accept short-term emergency placements, and had had only three, although each had lasted considerably longer than had originally been planned, which was often the way with short-term or emergency placements. We'd taken in an eight-year-old handful (to say the least) called Connor, then a little lad called Paulie whose mum and stepfather had rejected him, and another eight-year-old, very recently – over Christmas, in fact – who'd been in such terrible circumstances (her parents had groomed her to simulate sex acts on camera for a paedophile website) that, even with our lengthy experience of, and exposure to, the sharp end of life, we were still reeling from the very thought of what she'd been through.

So something like this, we agreed – be it for a short time or a longer one – would actually be a form of light relief.

'So they won't deport her?' Kieron wanted to know once he and Lauren had returned, and we'd explained why we had to leave in such a hurry. (Kieron would have happily shared the entire plot of the film with us otherwise, that being very much one of his favourite things.)

He seemed anxious to be sure about it, too. I shook my head. 'No. Well, certainly not at this stage. If she's homeless and a minor, the first thing will be to make sure she's safe, obviously. Plus she's an EU citizen, so she has rights here, in any case.'

Kieron unzipped his jacket. I could feel the cold coming off it. It was a bitterly cold evening. 'I knew it,' he said.

'Knew what, mate?' Mike asked him.

'I *knew* they didn't just deport people like that.'

'Well, they do in some cases …' I said. 'Depends very much on the circumstances. But in this case, of course not.

They first need to establish what she might be going back *to*. We don't yet know how she got here – even how long she's been here, come to that. Why, anyway?' I asked, curious.

'Oh, it's just there's this idiot at football I train with,' he said. 'He's a complete racist.' He glanced at Lauren. She obviously knew about this character already.

'Amongst other things …' she added. 'All-round nice guy, isn't he? We hear a lot about Idiot Ben,' she explained, smiling at me.

Kieron huffed. 'Because he *is* an idiot,' he said, shrugging the jacket off. 'Anyway, he was telling me they changed the laws so no one can come here any more.'

'I'm not sure he's right about that,' Mike commented, putting his own on. 'Though there's a fair few who'd agree with him, if they had.'

'But why?' Kieron seemed genuinely to want an explanation. 'I don't get it. We all live in Europe. We're all humans on the planet. And, anyway, no one stops *us* going to work *there*.'

'I'm not sure *working* there's the issue,' Mike said.

'Yes it is,' Kieron said. 'He's always banging on about how they take all our jobs.'

'When he's not banging on about them taking our benefits,' Lauren added drily.

'Except *do* they?' Kieron asked. 'And they can't do both, can they?'

Mike touched his arm. 'I'm with you there, son. Though I think that's a discussion for another day, don't you? We've got to get a move on or your mum'll start getting ants in her pants. There'll be at least a dozen specks of dust lurking that she'll have to send packing ...'

'Huh,' Kieron said. 'I flipping *knew* I was right. I really hate it when people assume I don't know anything about anything.'

'Which he will doubtless be addressing at the next football training session ...' I whispered to Mike as we hurried out of the door.

We returned home to find Tyler exactly where we'd left him – engrossed in the latest episode of *CSI: NY*, which was his latest 'must-see' TV show. And no sooner had we filled him in on our imminent young visitor than my mobile rang again, to alert us that the girl was now with John, and that, assuming we were okay with it, he'd be round with her in half an hour.

'It's a point, you know,' Mike said, once I'd delegated jobs, and sent Tyler off to the kitchen to do his washing up and generally straighten things up downstairs. 'You know, about her status here. Will she really be allowed to stay? What'll they do with her if she's got nobody and doesn't speak any English?'

'I have absolutely no idea,' I said. 'This is a new one on me, although I'm sure John knows the protocols. But I suppose at the moment, like we were saying, it's a case of a roof over her head, bless her. I wonder what her story is. I mean, how did she find her way here? She's a hell of a long way from home.'

My instinct was that that her being Polish would make no difference in the short term. There were generally two options with young people found on the street: the police would either take them home again or, if this was neither possible nor appropriate, call in social services to take over from there. In other cases, kids who'd run away to escape abuse became so exhausted and traumatised from not eating and not sleeping (or, worse, being beaten up or raped) that they'd take themselves to social services, pleased to be taken into care. It sounded like our young runaway fitted into the latter category, bless her.

'She's probably been trafficked,' decided Tyler, once he'd whizzed through his chores and come and joined us.

Mike chuckled as he went in search of bedding across the landing. 'And you'd know all about that, I suppose.'

'No, honest. I bet she has. They sneak them in through the Channel Tunnel under lorries. I saw a thing about it on telly the other week. What's she like, anyway? What's John said about her?'

'Almost nothing, love,' I told him. 'And no interrogations, okay? We're not in an episode of *CSI: NY*, remember. 'Here,' I added. 'Strip that duvet cover off for me, will you? I doubt *Frozen* is really going to be her thing. Mind you, I'm so out of touch these days with teenage girls that I'm not sure what her thing might actually be.'

'Well, I haven't done much better,' Mike called from his foray into the airing cupboard – an airing cupboard somewhat depleted as the result of one of my periodic New Year clear-outs, in preparation for a big shop in the January sales. Which I'd not quite got round to.

'It's basically a choice between Newcastle United and *The Little Mermaid*, currently,' Mike said, brandishing both sets in the bedroom doorway. 'Unless we put her in the double in the other spare room, but of course that means clearing all the junk out of it, of which there is a *lot* ...'

I stuck my tongue out at him, refusing to feel guilty about what I *had* managed to accomplish, which had been an overhaul and restock of my ever-expanding collection of toys. 'No, no time,' I said. '*The Little Mermaid* will have to do for now, I guess. Though I'm sure we had a simpler one. One with butterflies on. Oh God, surely all girls like mermaids?'

'That's sexist stereotyping, that is,' Tyler quipped. 'We just did it in PSE class. How d'you know she's not, like, a *massive* Newcastle fan?'

'That's a fair point,' I conceded. 'Though I suspect it might be wishful thinking on your part. Here. Grab the other end of that duvet – oh, but, God, that's a thought!'

'That sounds ominous,' Mike said. 'Go on then. What's a thought?'

'Polish! We don't know any, do we! How are we going to greet her? I'm going to have to go down and fire up the laptop before she arrives.'

'I do,' said Tyler. 'We've got those two Polish kids in my class, haven't I? Hang no – Mum, you've even met one. You know – Vladimir? Sooooo ... What do I know ... Erm ... Okay, here's one. "*Ziom*".'

'Come again?' said Mike.

'*Ziom*. It means bro,' explained Tyler. 'You know, like in "bruvva". As in, like, when you meet someone and you fist bump, and say, "Hey, bro – how's it hanging?"' He did a little fist bump with Mike to illustrate.

'Well, that's extremely helpful, I *don't* think,' I told him. 'I need "welcome" and "come in" and "This is your lovely temporary bedroom, but please don't read anything into *The Little Mermaid* duvet cover".'

I threw the last Ariel-emblazoned, half-in-its-case pillow at him. We needed all of that, yes, but mostly 'Don't be scared, love, you're safe now'. I left the bedroom and hurried down the stairs, suddenly remembering that Tyler would have probably left me a sinkful of dirty dishes and mugs to sort out as he'd been home alone for a couple of hours.

Chapter 2

The first thing I noticed about Adrianna was her hair. There was so much of it that it would have been impossible not to notice it: thick and wavy, it was the colour of a church pew or polished table and, though it was clearly in need of a good wash and brush, it was the sort of hair my mum would have called her 'crowning glory'. And it was long, falling down to her waist.

She was tall too – as girls often are at that age. A lot taller than I was – which wasn't hard, admittedly. She was also painfully skinny, but though she looked exhausted and in need of a good meal, there was no denying her natural beauty.

'Come in, come in,' I urged, gesturing with my hand that she should do so, trying to reassure her, despite knowing that there was little I could say – in any language – that would make her less terrified than she so obviously was. Not yet, anyway. I knew she was a child still but I doubted there was a person of any age who'd find anything about her current situation easy.

In common with so many of the children Mike and I took in, Adrianna had arrived with barely anything. She had a small and obviously very old leather handbag, the strap for which she held protectively, like a shield. Other than the bag – and it could have barely housed more than a purse and passport – she appeared only to have the clothes she stood up in. A pair of sturdy boots – again, elderly – and of a Doc Martens persuasion, a long corduroy skirt in a deep berry shade, a roll-neck black jumper and a leather biker jacket, which, once again, had clearly seen better days.

And all of it just that little bit too big for her. So, on the face of it she should have looked like the refugee she purported to be, but instead she had the bearing and grace of a model. It was only her eyes that betrayed her anxiety and desperation. I found myself wondering two things – first, when she might have last had a bath or a shower, and second, what kind of background she had come from. Bedraggled as she was, I knew that those boots and that jacket wouldn't have been cheap.

'So,' said John, herding her in but never quite making contact – I sensed a strong reluctance on his part to try to baby her too much. 'No luck with an interpreter, so we're just going to have to make the best of it tonight, I'm afraid. I've left a message with head office and made it clear that it's urgent, so hopefully we'll have better luck getting hold of someone tomorrow morning. In the meantime –'

'In the meantime, you look frozen,' I said to Adrianna, grabbing her free hand impulsively and seeing the fear widen her eyes. I let her go again, smiling, trying to keep reassuring her. 'Look at you,' I said again, now rubbing my hands up and down my own arms. 'A hot drink, I think. Coffee? *Kawa*? Tea?'

'*Kawa, dzieki. Dzieki*,' she answered.

'Thank you,' said Tyler, who was standing with Mike behind me. '*Dzieki* means thank you,' he explained, smiling shyly. And he was rewarded by the ghost of a smile in return.

I took her hand again and this time I grasped it more firmly. 'You're welcome,' I said, squeezing it to underline my words.

'*Dzieki*,' she said again, her eyes glinting with tears now. 'Dzieki. *Dzieki. Dzieki.*'

In the event, there was no need for an extended session of complicated, halting, hand-gesture conversation because all Adrianna wanted to do was go to bed. Once she'd gulped down her coffee – and she really did gulp it – she almost bit my hand off when I gestured we might go upstairs.

And I understood that. I had no idea how far she'd travelled or what sort of trauma she'd run away from, but the need to shut the world out is a universal one.

'So, this is the bathroom,' I explained needlessly once we'd arrived on the landing, leaving Mike and John downstairs to deal with the paperwork. Tyler, too, seemed to understand he'd be better off leaving us to it. Having exhausted the little stock of useful Polish that he knew, he'd quickly announced he was off to spend some time on Google Translate and disappeared into his own bedroom.

'Make yourself at home,' I said to Adrianna, gesturing again, this time towards the bottles of shower gel and shampoo. 'Have a bath, if you want. I've sorted out some clean nightclothes and put them on your bed ...'

To which the same response came – *dzieki*, *dzieki*. She didn't seem to want to attempt to say anything else.

'So, anyway, your bedroom ...' I began, stepping back out, assuming she'd follow me, but no sooner had I left the bathroom than she had her hand on the door.

'*Prosze*,' she said. '*Prosze*?' She frowned and bobbed slightly. A brief knock-kneed curtsey, accompanied by a grimace.

I grinned, the penny dropping. And then the thought of the word 'penny' made my grin turn to a chuckle. Some things were the same in any language.

Back downstairs I joined John and Mike at the dining table, the piece of furniture across which so many similar discussions had taken place over the years, and so many pieces of paper shunted back and forth for signing – the placement plans, the risk assessments, the parental consent forms, to name but a few. Though, on some occasions, this one included, the paperwork was secondary – the main aim was to find a home, and fast.

Because Adrianna had come to us as an emergency placement, there was no care plan yet in place for her, of course. Or, indeed, a social worker allocated to her. We were just, as John had already told us, a place of safety for her to be billeted at while investigations were made into her situation – for which we'd obviously need that interpreter – and the circumstances that had brought her to us. As a 14-year-old there was no question of her going to supported lodgings placement; she needed full-time carers, as well as an education. Not to mention health care, which would obviously include a doctor and a dentist, as well as access to an optician and a school nurse. These things were standard in the UK, of course, but I knew nothing of the system from which Adrianna had come.

All this, however, was to be arranged down the line. In the short term we urgently needed an interpreter, which, once the little paperwork we could deal with was quickly dispatched, John promised he would return with the following morning.

'Well, in theory,' he said, as he put his papers away and prepared to leave us. 'It's just occurred to me that our usual woman is away on holiday, so it might prove to be much easier said than actually done. If so, I guess it's going to have to be Google Translate!'

In the end it wasn't necessary for us to break out the laptop, because just as he'd hoped, John was back with an interpreter the following morning, just after Tyler – much disgruntled – had already left for school. He'd already, it seemed, taken quite a shine to our latest family member, and was disappointed that I hadn't dragged her from her bed before he went.

And 'dragged' was the operative word. I showed the men into the usual seats around the dining table then hotfooted it upstairs to wake Adrianna before making coffee, thankful for the ten-minute warning John had texted (which had at least given *me* time to dress), having the previous evening told me they'd be coming around ten.

And, boy, she took some waking. With the curtains shut tight, and her burrowed completely under the duvet, it was like walking into a tomb. And when she did wake and I explained they'd come earlier than expected, she showed zero enthusiasm for getting up and meeting her new interrogator, even when I indicated that she could do so in her dressing gown, not least because 8.45 a.m. was a very teenager-unfriendly time of day at the best of times. And these were definitely not the best of times.

I couldn't say I blamed her. Though I didn't yet know how long she'd been sleeping rough (something, among many other things, that I now aimed to find out), there was still the small matter that she'd travelled several hundred miles the previous day, was unwell, among strangers, and with her future uncertain. I think I'd have preferred to stay in bed as well.

'I'm sorry,' John said, as I returned to the dining room and promised that Adrianna would be down shortly. 'It's just that Mr Kanski here is on a tight schedule today and it was a question of making hay while the sun shone.'

'That's fine,' I reassured him. 'What would you both like to drink?'

'Er, nothing,' John answered, glancing at the other man before speaking. 'Tight for time, as I say …'

'Up to you,' I said. 'But I'm having one. It won't take long, and –' I indicated upstairs with a nod.

But the man shook his head. 'No, thanks all the same,' he answered stiffly.

I went out into the kitchen, catching John's eye as I left. Looking at Mr Kanski, I'd had that thing happen. That thing – thankfully it only happens to me rarely – where a person does something – some small thing; it's often not a big thing – to make you form an unfavourable first impression. There was nothing about Mr Kanski that I could really put my finger on. He was the sort of unremarkable, soberly dressed man I'd half-expected. Late thirties, perhaps, or early forties. The sort of person who wouldn't really make any sort of impression if they were sitting beside you on a bus. But there was something that set my teeth on edge about him nevertheless. He wasn't exactly impolite but then he wasn't exactly on the same page as me either. I got no sense that Adrianna's desperate circumstances particularly moved him, even though I felt absolutely sure John would have conveyed the distressing nature of them to him on the way here. Plus there was this sense I had – strongly – that some words had been exchanged between them. That 'fitting us in' was some major inconvenience.

As well it might be, I thought, as I popped my head out of the kitchen door and hollered 'Adrianna, how are you doing?' up the stairs. I did it as much for the man's benefit as anything. It might well be that he had much bigger translation fish to fry and that coming to chat to our 14-year-old runaway was indeed a bit of a pain.

Even so it rankled and, as I came out of the kitchen to see Adrianna starting down the stairs, I nodded towards the living-room door and pulled a conspirator's face – just a very slight one – to let her know he seemed a grumpy old sod.

Of course, what Adrianna made of all my gurning could only be guessed at, but it was an irrelevance in any case, because as soon as we all gathered at the table I could see, just by her body language, that she felt the same about him as I did.

And she dealt with it in the traditional teenagerly way, by switching off. You could almost hear the click. And what she started with her expression, she finished with her body language; she didn't so much sit, as slither down into the dining chair, sitting back, looking across the table with tired, wary eyes. Quite apart from anything else, she looked ill. Definitely as if she was still running a temperature, and I had to fight an impulse to reach across and place the flat of my hand against her head. Perhaps having the man round for an interrogation so soon wasn't a very good idea. It wasn't as if there was some huge rush to all this, after all. It wasn't like anybody was going anywhere.

John cleared his throat and adjusted his tie. 'Adrianna, this is Mr Kanski,' he explained, a little over-brightly. 'He's come to help with the translation of our conversation.' And as if via autocue, because I didn't see any sort of sign pass between them, Mr Kanski duly translated what he said. I had to admit, he seemed good at it.

'So,' John continued, 'we need to find out a little more about you, Adrianna. Then we will know how best to help you. Is that okay?'

The man began translating this as well, and, seeing Adrianna's glazed expression, I decided to help things along a bit by getting her some pills.

'Sorry,' I said, as he glanced irritably at me, 'I just want to pop into the kitchen and grab Adrianna some water and paracetamol. She's not very well,' I added, looking at Mr Kanski. He nodded. 'But please feel free to carry on without me,' I added. 'I'm aware that time's an issue.'

Smiling politely, I then got up and left the room.

I was gone no time at all – couldn't have been much more than a couple of minutes – but by the time I returned John had already scribbled a fair bit on his pad. I couldn't see what, but as I put the tablets and water in front of Adrianna I could sense a definite tension in the room.

The translator was speaking again, obviously reiterating some lengthy question John had put to her while I was in the kitchen, and as he spoke I could see Adrianna already forming a head shake. And then another. Then a shoulder shrug and spread of her palms.

'*Nie*,' she said. Followed by an indecipherable longer utterance.

'She says she has no family to go back to,' the man said. 'She said she is an orphan. She says she doesn't know when or where she entered the UK.'

'No family at *all*?' John asked. 'Was she brought up in care, then?'

The man asked her. Again, no. 'She says a children's home. In Krakow. Which she ran away from.'

I looked across at Adrianna. Despite the direness of her straits and her obvious infection, one thing I'd noticed straight away was her unmistakable sense of self. Her self-possession. Her bearing. This was a child raised in the care system? It didn't seem to fit. I knew they came in all shapes and sizes – as did all kids – but there was always this look they had; of being beaten down, diminished. Faintly hostile. Assessing. Adrianna just *didn't*. She just didn't *look* like a looked-after child. 'So no family whatsoever?' I asked, looking quizzically at her.

Mr Kanski asked the question again. Adrianna looked right back at me as she answered. And provided another '*Nie*'.

'So how about your time in the UK?' John continued, with his pen poised over a pad, ready to spring into action. 'Can you tell me more about that? What have you been doing? How have you been living? With friends? On the streets? Have you been staying in any hostels? Have you had any contact with social services, or the housing office, there?'

Adrianna listened, seemingly intently, because she sat slightly forwards as Mr Kanski conveyed all this. Then she responded with another lengthy stream of Polish. But even as she spoke I knew we were making little in the way of progress. It was just so obvious, from her tone, from the lack of place names, from the wealth of 'ums' and 'ers' and shrugs, so when Mr Kanski explained that she'd been 'getting by', living on friends' floors and couldn't remember any details about anywhere she'd been staying as she'd always 'moved around a lot', it came as no sort of surprise. She clearly wanted to tell us as little as possible.

'What friends?' I asked. 'Are there friends who'll be wondering where you are now, Adrianna?' I asked, speaking directly to her.

'No one,' came Mr Kanski's answer, in translation of yet another flat '*Nie*'.

'What about London, Adrianna? Where you've just come from? How long were you there?' John asked. 'You were there for a bit, weren't you? Before you arrived in Hull?'

'About a month, she thinks,' Mr Kanski said, once he'd asked the question and been given the answer. 'Though, I think –'

'Casey?' Adrianna's voice. Small but decisive. 'I not so good.' She gestured to her head and grimaced at me. 'Ill.'

And to be fair, she certainly looked it. Her face was pale and clammy and her hair was sticking to her forehead. 'You know what?' I said to John. 'I think we should hold off doing this until Adrianna's feeling a little better, don't you? Come on, love,' I said, rising from my seat and gesturing that she should also. 'Back to bed with you.' I turned to John. 'We can just as easily have this conversation in a few days, can't we? And with Mr Kanski in a hurry to be somewhere anyway, perhaps that's best, eh? I'm sure we'll be able to get more out of her once she's properly rested and feeling brighter ...' I moved aside to let Adrianna pass me.

She even smelt unwell. Not as in body odour particularly. Just that slightly rank, sick-roomy smell. 'Off you go, sweetheart,' I said gently. 'Oh, and take your water with you. I'll be up to see how you're doing in a bit, okay?'

'*Dzieki*,' she said. '*Dzieke*.' Then she was gone from the room.

Both men watched her leave, though with different expressions. I got the feeling that Mr Kanski was only a whisker short of huffing about being dragged round in the first place. 'Well, we tried,' John said, clicking his ballpoint and putting his pad away. 'But you're right, Casey. Best we leave all this for a bit, I think. If you're happy to hang on to her, that is.'

I rolled my eyes at him. 'You *know* I am, John. Don't be silly. Anyway,' I said, eyeing the pad that was disappearing back into his briefcase, 'what did you manage to get? You know, while I was out in the kitchen.'

'Nothing,' he said. 'She's proving to be a dark horse, this one, isn't she?'

Mr Kanski kind of rustled. John noted it. 'And thanks so much for coming at such short notice, Robert,' he said to the other man. 'It really is much appreciated, even if we didn't manage to get very far.'

'Which is understandable,' I added. 'I should really have called you and stopped you coming. I would have, had I realised soon enough. She's clearly got some sort of virus, bless her ...'

Which was when I got that sense of it again with Mr Kanski. Just a slight tweak in expression, the sense of words thought but unspoken. 'Well, that may be so,' he said, glancing at me through narrowed eyes. 'But she's lying through her teeth.' He smiled a grim, humourless smile, which included both of us. 'But I imagine you already knew that.' He put a fist to his mouth and cleared his throat. 'Anyway, nothing unusual there, eh?'

He checked the clock on his mobile, then slipped it into his coat pocket. 'Shall we, John?'

It was awkward, and strange, and I pondered it as I saw them out. Even with John's light-hearted, even jocular 'You got it – in our line of work that's pretty much a given!' there was *something*. Like there was something we didn't know about *him*.

'You know what? I should invite Vlad to tea tomorrow, shouldn't I?' Tyler, home from school and football practice, had obviously been giving the language barrier serious thought. 'I was thinking it would probably be better – you know, like in she might open up more, if she could speak to someone Polish who's her own age. Not some old, disapproving crusty,' he added, causing me to stifle a chuckle. I had, of course, filled him in as much as was appropriate. Perhaps *too* much, I decided, pressing the chuckle down.

'You know, that isn't a bad idea,' Mike said, holding his hands out for Tyler's filthy football boots. One of my most favourite rituals in a relationship that seemed to thrive on them was Mike's undying devotion to cleaning Tyler's muddy boots. It was a kind of symbiosis, even – it meant Tyler felt loved and cared for (which he was) and also filled the Kieron's-football-boot-shaped hole in Mike's life. On such seemingly small things are great strides so often made.

'I know,' Tyler said. 'And he's stoked about meeting her. Shall I text him?'

'Hold your horses, love,' I cautioned. 'Let's be sensible. One, she's not well – and it's probably contagious – and two, she might not be quite up to meeting Vlad yet.' I spoke with feeling, Vlad being one of the more memorable of Tyler's friends. He was a big lad, in all ways – he had a big personality, and also found it difficult to cross a room without knocking something over. Not so much uncoordinated as a force of nature, barely contained. 'Tell you what. Keep him on standby. Tell him we'd love to have him over, but that we'll hold off till next week, when whatever this bug is has run its course. Which I'm sure it will.'

Mike ran a hand over his throat. 'Hmm. If we're lucky.'

And we were lucky – well, in the short term, as whatever it was didn't seem to touch us. But Adrianna herself continued to be really poorly. She spent the remainder of Wednesday in bed – only surfacing to sit with us in the living room to watch David Attenborough for an hour that evening, and barely got out of it at all on Thursday.

'You know what I'm going to do?' I said to Mike before he left for work on Friday morning. 'I'm going to call the GP surgery and see if I can get a home visit. I think she's poorly. As in sick. With a virus or something. Which I know he won't be able to help with,' I added, before Mike could. (He was something of a pedant when it came to

25

people going to doctors when they had viruses, having seen a programme on telly about how the over-prescription of antibiotics was causing all the terrifying superbugs in the world.) 'I just think it wouldn't hurt for her to have a bit of a once-over, would it? Specially if she's been sleeping rough for a while. And she's so *thin*. And let's face it, we don't know the first thing about what she's been up to or who she's been with. She could have *anything* wrong with her, couldn't she?'

'No, I think that's a good idea, love,' he said. 'Put our minds at rest, too. We can't just keep feeding her paracetamols, can we? She needs to be up and eating. Can't be doing her any good, being holed up in that bedroom morning, noon and night, can it?'

Which sentiment I agreed with, even given the usual teenage propensity for sleeping the day away. Adrianna, however, seemed to have other ideas.

'No, no. Am ok-*ay*,' she assured me when I went up to suggest it mid-morning, Tyler having long since left for school. 'Am ok-ay. No problem.' She rubbed sleep out of her eyes. 'Please. No doctor.'

But there was no dissuading me, not least because of the uneaten sandwich from the previous evening currently curling on the bedside table, the sheen of sweat on her brow and the faint but still palpable smell in the room. It wasn't exactly fetid, in the usual teenage-boy's-trainer-pile kind of way. Just distinctive and familiar. A smell every mother learns to recognise. The smell of sick child. Of fever and sweat – of malaise.

And something else. Something familiar but which I couldn't quite put my finger on. A sweetish smell. Odd. Definitely not right. '*Yes* doctor,' I said firmly, picking up the plate and the empty mug beside it. If there was one thing she *could* clearly stomach, it was coffee. 'Just to check you *are* okay,' I added gently. At which she pushed back the duvet.

'I get up,' she said. 'Am okay. See? No doctor. I have bat?'

It took me a second. Then she pointed towards the bathroom and I realised. 'Bath?'

She swung her legs out of bed and stood up, her pale feet looking stark against the hot pink of her pyjama bottoms. 'Bath,' she confirmed, nodding. 'I have bath. Am okay, Casey. No doctor.'

I stood aside so she could pluck her fleecy dressing gown – formerly Riley's – from the back of the dressing-table chair. 'I don't know, love …' I began, my mind now filling with a whole new set of questions. Why the great reluctance to see a doctor? What did she imagine he'd do to her? Was it a reticence born out of fear of further questioning by someone in authority? She was clearly terrified of being sent away again, after all. Or did she have something else to hide – something physical, that she didn't want him to see? Scarring, perhaps? Bruising? I couldn't help but wonder because, these days, such thoughts kicked in so automatically; I'd seen so many damaged children – as in burned, battered and beaten – that now it was an instant response in me. Where *had* she come from? *Had* she perhaps been abused?

27

'*Dzieki*,' she said, as she hurried across the landing and went into the bathroom.

'Adrianna!' I called before she slammed the door. I'd just had another thought and slipped into the bathroom as she stood there looking surprised. I opened the bathroom cabinet and gestured with my hand that she should look, so that she could see I had a stock of sanitary protection in there, just in case. I could have kicked myself – perhaps that was all it was after all. She was the right age, and if I remembered correctly, Riley had suffered terribly with her periods as a young teenager – cramps, fatigue and a roaring temperature. Why hadn't that occurred to me before now?

I went downstairs and called the doctor anyway.

Chapter 3

Though we'd moved twice in the last decade, we'd stayed with the same GP surgery, not least because Dr Shakelton, who was now approaching (his long overdue) retirement and only working part-time, was such a brilliant and caring GP. Just not an available one right this minute, as it turned out. Despite it being one of his days in the surgery, he was off work with a virus himself. So the doctor who appeared on our doorstep at the end of morning surgery was one of the newer partners, a young, fresh-faced GP I'd seen a couple of times around the surgery but had never had any dealings with before. Stepping into the hall, he introduced himself just as 'Joe', in the modern way they usually did now.

He looked like a Joe, too. Bright and friendly and approachable. 'She's not a refugee, exactly,' I explained to him, once we'd dispensed with the usual pleasantries and I'd given him the lowdown on why Adrianna had come to us. 'She's been in the country a while now, as far as we know

– albeit under the radar – and she's by all accounts Polish, which makes her an EU national obviously. But she's not well. Hasn't been right since she came to us. She spends most of her time sleeping, and lives off little more than coffee and paracetamol. And she's definitely feverish.'

Joe nodded. 'Any vomiting?'

I shook my head. 'Not that I know of. I'm sure not, in fact. I'm a bit of a sleuth like that,' I added, grinning. 'You get to be in my line of work. So I'm pretty sure I'd know if she had been sick. And no light sensitivity, either. And no rash, as far as I can see. Though I have actually managed to see very little of her.' I spread my hands. 'So it might be nothing – well, nothing more than a mild virus, anyway. Or she might just be exhausted – she probably is. Or depressed – that was my other thought. And then it's just occurred to me that it might simply be that time of the month and she's too embarrassed, or doesn't have the language to tell me. It's so hard when you don't speak the same language, isn't it? And there was no way in the *world* I'd be able to coax her down to the surgery …'

'So the surgery has come to her,' Joe the GP reassured me, grinning back at me as he hefted his heavy case. 'Though I must confess I don't speak much Polish myself. I was trying to think of a some words in the car on the way over – I do have a few Polish patients, so I'm not entirely clueless. I know "*Polski*", of course – much use that's going to be – and "*czemu*", which means "why", and "*nie rozumiem*", which is Polish – or so I'm told – for "I don't understand".' He laughed as he shrugged off his jacket and began rolling up his shirt sleeves. 'Which both come up quite a lot, as you can imagine. But which aren't going to be a whole lot of use to us, are they? But that's okay. Let's take a look at her. That's the main thing. Check her over. Upstairs, I presume?'

'Upstairs,' I confirmed, leading the way up the stairs. 'And, doctor, I'm so sorry if it's something and nothing and I've got you here on a wild goose chase.'

'Oh, think nothing of it,' he said, smiling. I decided I liked Dr Joe.

Adrianna was back in bed again when I pushed the bedroom door fully open, having noted the welcome development that at least she had left it ajar. She was a small S shape under the covers, curled up with her head facing the wall, and her hair, which was obviously still wet from her bath, gathered up inside a turban of towel.

'Sweetie,' I said softly as I entered, 'are you awake?'

Clearly yes. She turned over to face me with a wan smile. Then saw the doctor behind me and stiffened.

'It's okay,' I soothed. 'Now, I know you don't think you need to see a doctor, but you're not well, and I'm afraid I don't agree. So here he is ...'

I trailed off then, conscious both of the anxiety on her face and the fact that she probably only understood one word in four. If that. Which made my twittering pretty pointless. It made me suddenly remember watching a foreign film with Mike one evening. It was subtitled but something went wrong with the TV while we were watching and the subtitles disappeared. It was a strange experience watching something and trying to follow the plot, when all the time the background sounds of people talking in a different language actually put you off what was happening.

'Hello, Adrianna,' Joe said brightly, stepping round me. 'I'm Joe. I'm a doctor. And I hear you're feeling poorly. I've come to see how you're doing. Is that okay?'

He didn't seem to care that she could barely understand him. And he probably had a point, because some things are universal, aren't they? His bright but brisk tone was saying it for him well enough. And though I knew she probably couldn't understand many of the actual words, Adrianna shuffled herself up to a sitting position and made her own feelings known by pulling the duvet up to her chin, her eyes darting mistrustfully between the doctor and me. It was a reaction that only heightened my sense of her anguish and dislocation. Where were her parents? Where were her loved ones? Why was she so far from home?

I remained in the doorway, nodding encouragement and watching as the doctor said 'May I?' and then plonked himself down at the edge of the single bed. Adrianna pulled her legs up even further.

'*Polski*?' Joe said, placing his bag down by his feet and opening it. Adrianna nodded, her eyes following his every movement.

'And not much English?' Joe continued. 'So we'll have to do our best with each other, won't we? So, what I'm going to do is take your temperature –' He pulled an ear thermometer from his bag. 'You've seen one of these?'

The gesture he made with it was obvious enough, and Adrianna nodded.

'I'd like to use this to take your temperature. In your ear,' he explained, indicating his own. 'Like this. Is that okay?'

Adrianna nodded again, albeit reluctantly, and allowed the doctor to place the thermometer in her ear, pulling the towel off as she did so and letting her hair coil down her back.

'Well, it's certainly up,' Joe said, after the machine beeped its answer. 'High, but not dangerously so. So, most importantly, how do you *feel*?' he asked Adrianna, making gestures as he did so. 'Do you feel sick?' He indicated this using two fingers. 'Any stomach pain?' Rubbing his own and pulling a face. 'Does your head hurt?' He pressed his hand to his temple and groaned. 'Dizzy?' He made a brief spinning motion with his hand. 'How about your chest?' he asked finally, placing a hand across his own chest and coughing.

To all of which, Adrianna, looking scared and suspicious, performed a series of equally clear responses. Head shakes, emphatic ones, to each enquiry. No. 'I am tired,' she said finally. 'I am okay. I am tired.'

'Perhaps because you're *sick*, Adrianna,' Joe persisted. He made another gesture, placing his palms together and raising them to his cheek. 'To be so tired. Not good. So I need to examine you …' He reached down again, to uncurl a stethoscope from his bag. 'Check your chest. Check your stomach. Check your skin for any rashes …'

'Should I leave you?' I asked, conscious of Adrianna's right to privacy. Her gaze shifted to me immediately, even though I doubted she understood what I'd said.

Joe looked at her enquiringly, then back again at me. 'I'm sure you can st–' he began.

'But I am *fine*,' Adrianna said again. She clutched the duvet even closer to her chin, as if to underline the point.

'It's nothing to be afraid of,' Joe said reassuringly, placing the ear buds in his ears. 'I just need a little listen of your chest and back with this. That's all. Nothing to worry about. But if you'd like Casey to leave us …'

'No touch!' It came out almost as a shriek, making me jump. Like a noise made by a cornered, frightened animal.

Which, in effect, was what she was. At least, in her mind. 'Sweetheart, it's *okay*,' I said. 'You've nothing to fear, I promise. The doctor just wants to –'

'No touch!' Almost a scream now. 'No touch me! Am *fine*!'

'Adrianna –' Joe began. Arianna's hand flew towards the stethoscope, batting it angrily away from her, making the end flip up and hit the doctor on the arm.

'No TOUCH me!'

'Sweetheart,' I tried, coming closer. She looked genuinely terrified. 'What's all this *about*? The doctor just needs to –'

'No touch me! No TOUCH me!' she yelled. Proper screams now.

Joe put his hands up. 'Okay, okay. No touch. I promise. I'm not here to hurt you, Adrianna. Just to see if you need help. Need *medicine* perhaps. Medicine?' he repeated, enunciating the word carefully. 'You understand "medicine"? In case you're ill?' He raised the stethoscope again, and again Adrianna batted her hand at it. So he lowered it, then placed it back in his bag and raised his empty hands. 'All right. Fair enough then. Perhaps we'll leave that for another day.'

'No TOUCH,' Adrianna sobbed. 'Am ok-AY! Am ok-AY!'

Which pretty much confirmed it. She wasn't.

'Perhaps,' Joe said once we were back downstairs again, 'this is best left till she can be seen by someone who can communicate with her properly. I'll ask Dr Shakelton if he can fit her in, shall I? He has quite a few Polish patients, and might be able to reassure her.'

I didn't say so but I doubted it. Whatever had caused Adrianna's outburst struck me as being less to do with the language barrier than with the gender barrier, which only reinforced my increasing worry that there was more going on than simple displacement or fear of strangers.

And it seemed Dr Joe was thinking along the same lines. 'You know, something else strikes me,' he said, just as I was about to suggest it. 'Perhaps she'd be better off seeing a female GP. Perhaps that's it. Perhaps that's the way forward. Though, for what it's worth, I'm not unduly concerned about her physically. Yes, her temperature is a little high, but I've not seen anything to ring alarm bells. She's pale, yes, and she definitely looks run down, as you say, but I

35

don't think she's confused. I suggest you keep a close eye on her and if you're in the least bit anxious call the surgery again, or bring her down, of course – or I'll come back to her. Or call an ambulance,' he finished. 'You know the drill.'

I nodded as I passed him his jacket. 'I think there is probably a great deal we don't know,' I said. 'And I think you might be right. Though on the face of it, I think I might need CAMHS more than I need a GP right now. I'm sorry to have called you out for nothing.'

CAMHS was the Child and Adolescent Mental Health Service, and I made a mental note to ask John what he thought about involving them with Adrianna. But even as I thought it, I doubted they would see her as a priority, knowing their workload, which was always immense. They tended to be more involved with children with behavioural problems rather than linguistic barriers.

'No, no. You did the right thing,' Dr Joe said as he rolled his sleeves down and pulled his jacket back on. 'I'm inclined to think it's a viral infection, so I won't prescribe anything just yet – not without taking a proper look at her – but I agree with you; it might be worth you looking into some sort of counselling service – preferably one with a translator. I don't know what you've been thinking but I wonder if her reaction to me could be a sign of some kind of abuse?' He frowned. 'I mean, if she's a runaway and has been sleeping rough ... Well, it's not exactly unlikely, after all.'

I told him I'd been thinking exactly the same thing and that I was going to speak to John Fulshaw as soon as I'd logged his visit. 'And in the meantime,' I asked, 'should I give her anything at all? You know, for her temperature or anything?'

'Just paracetamol if she appears to need it, and obviously keep her well hydrated, but, seriously, if she's no better by Monday, do give me another call and we'll see what we can conjure. And, as I say, call the out-of-hours service over the weekend if you're concerned. It's always better to be over-cautious when there's a language barrier. She might not know the words to tell us what's wrong, mightn't she?'

And more to the point, I thought – but didn't say, since the doctor had a busy afternoon ahead of him – didn't seem to *want* to find the words to do so either, which struck me as the oddest thing of all.

I went straight back upstairs as soon as the doctor had left, to find Adrianna where we'd left her, curled up under the duvet, seemingly unwilling to ever relinquish it again. Was that her plan? To just stay there till someone commanded her to go elsewhere? What was going *on* in this enigmatic teenage girl's head?

'*Przepraszam*,' she said quietly. 'Casey, I am sorry.'

I didn't need the translation. I knew what *przepraszam* meant because Tyler had already told me (though it sounded like a spell off *Harry Potter*). It was one of the words on the list he had painstakingly written out for me. A list of words and phrases, I noted, that he had also copied for Adrianna in reverse, but which, these few instances of courtesy aside, she seemed to have little interest in studying.

She had little interest in improving her English at all, it seemed. Why? Since she didn't seem to want to go home, why wouldn't she?

I experienced a moment of frustration. This was surely one of the ways in which she (and immigrants generally) could only strengthen her position. I knew what people could be like. You saw it everywhere. It genuinely irritated people when immigrants appeared not to want to integrate; a point of view with which I had sympathy.

But this poor child – for child she was – obviously had a great deal more going on in that head of hers than we knew, and now was probably not the moment to start grilling her about her lack of vocabulary. She'd been with us less than a week. She was scared and traumatised, and also suffering from a probable virus. So what harm was there in her sleeping the days away till she was well enough to see past that? At least the doctor had been, and his reassurance had done its job and reassured *me*.

'It's okay, love,' I told her, patting her. 'I just don't understand, that's all.' I smiled. 'But you don't understand me either, do you? So there's not much point in me rattling on at you, is there? You get some sleep now.' I mimicked the praying movement the doctor had made earlier, then pointed floorwards. 'I'll be downstairs if you need me.'

And, in the meantime, I would go down and log the doctor's visit. And perhaps call John Fulshaw to see how he felt we should best proceed. Because, for all that this was seemingly a clear, temporary brief (and to which my usual

'Yes I can' response still felt like the right one), something was beginning to make me think there'd be complications down the line. In short, my fostering antennae were now twitching.

And they continued to do so as I sat at the dining table typing on my laptop, coffee at my side, pondering the question of quite what to do next. I could hardly get online and teach myself Polish in a couple of hours, just as surely as I couldn't teach Adrianna English – even should she express any enthusiasm for learning it. Not that I should get ahead of myself; the answer to the question might equally be 'nothing', as John might call any day to announce she was leaving, having found a suitable foster family for her long-term. Or, less likely, but still one of a range of possibilities, a friendly relative who'd popped out of the woodwork and come to take her home.

In the meantime we could only keep on doing what we were doing, and – in my case, because it was *my* antennae that were twitching – be alert to anything that might shed more light on our secretive girl's situation.

I was just committing that thought to the keyboard when I heard the front door, closely followed by a shouted 'Cooooeee! Get the kettle on, sis!'

I smiled and lowered the screen on the laptop. We'd had one of those huge budget supermarkets open at the end of our road the previous year – a circumstance that had caused quite a lot of disgruntlement among the neighbours, for fear of parking issues, littering and a general 'lowering of the tone', as if we were some posh middle-class suburb, which we weren't. Even so, there was the usual snobbish annoyance at the council for letting them do it, something which, not being as perfect as we liked to believe, myself and Mike – ahem – were a part.

It didn't take long, though, to realise how silly we'd been. For starters, we soon realised we were saving a fortune, and, better still, it meant I saw more of my sister.

Donna ran a café in town – had done for a few years now. And a very good café it was too. She'd called it Truly Scrumptious, and the fare she served obviously was, because it was heaving pretty much every day of the week. And with the new branch of the budget supermarket being so close to us, she could grab a cab there – she didn't drive – and stock up on super-cheap tea, coffee and sugar, and then drop in for a coffee and a natter with me and, sometimes, a lift back as well.

I got up to find her in the hall, plonking down a load of straining carrier bags. 'Only a quick one,' she clarified. 'I've just got half an hour. Carol's in on her own, and I've dragged Chloe in to help, so I'd better be quick.'

Carol was the stalwart who'd worked for Donna almost since the outset, and Chloe was my 18-year-old niece. She was in the sixth form, and, in theory, was only supposed to work on Saturdays, but if it was a day when she didn't have any lessons, and the café was busy, Donna would often let her come in and earn a bit of extra pocket money.

'So. Where is she?' Donna asked without preamble. My sister didn't foster, but she always took an interest. So much so that I hadn't ruled out the possibility that, if the café ever became too much or too samey, that at some point she too might take the plunge.

I indicated with my eyes as I poured us both a coffee. 'Upstairs in bed. She's not well. So there's not much to report. She's barely been downstairs since she came here.'

'But she's a teenager, isn't she?' Donna said. 'So that's just typical. Teenagers like hiding away in their bedrooms. I wouldn't worry – you hardly ever see them at that age.'

'I don't think that's it in this instance,' I said. 'She's not right. She's not right and she's ill too.'

I told Donna about the doctor's visit and Adrianna's extreme, and unexpected, reaction to it. She laughed. She used the same surgery that we did. 'Dr Joe? Well, he'd get quite the opposite reaction from *me*. Though, to be fair, she *is* 14. You know what girls are like at that age. Some strange man comes in, starts wanting to prod her around – and a foreigner, to boot … Seriously, what's the story with her? I'm completely intrigued. I didn't realise you could even foster foreign nationals. Stuff you hear about them being taken to detention centres and all that.'

I laughed. 'Hardly – she's from Poland. So she's allowed to be here anyway. Well, would be, if she was here legally. Which we're not sure she is. She says she doesn't even have a passport. But, to be honest, we know almost nothing else about her. We've barely exchanged half a dozen sentences the entire time she's been with us, and, as I say, her English is almost non-existent. And not likely to improve, either – she seems frightened of everybody and everything, wouldn't answer any of the interpreter's questions, wouldn't let Tyler bring his Polish friend home for tea, and, well, as I say, just seems to want to stay in bed, pretty much. Right now I don't know whether she's properly sick, or homesick, or just plain exhausted. And there doesn't seem a lot I can do about any of it at present either. Which is a pretty odd place for me to be.' I glanced across at my fridge freezer. 'Sounds mad, but I'm missing my chart!'

Donna grinned. Then said thoughtfully, 'It's probably a combination of all of those things, isn't it? And it's only been a few days, after all. You can't expect to know everything about everything after such a short time. Even *you*.'

'That's what Mike thinks,' I said. 'But you know when you just have that inkling about someone? Well, I've got that. Increasingly, that's what I've got.'

'Such as?'

'Such as despite what she told John, I reckon there's something bad, as in possibly actionable, that she's run away from. And not back in Poland, either. I reckon there's more. Something criminal. Something *serious*.' I tapped the table top. 'Something that's happened *here*. Maybe she's witnessed something. Some crime or something. You know?'

Donna drained her mug. 'You watch too many bloody Scandinavian murder mysteries, you do. Anyway, speaking of criminal, can you whistle up one of those over-priced taxis for me? I'm assuming a lift home's probably not on the cards.'

'Poland's not in Scandinavia,' I pointed out. 'And, no, sorry, sis – you know I would but I don't like to leave her. I just have this suspicion –'

'Go on, tell me. That there might be bogeymen lurking behind Lidl, and that things are not entirely az zey seeeem?'

At which I laughed, because I knew my imagination *could* get the better of me. But that, or a version of it – that Adrianna was running scared – was almost exactly what I *did* think.

Chapter 4

Thankfully, over the weekend Adrianna's temperature went down and by Sunday she had ventured downstairs to join the family, clad in a hoodie and old trackie bottoms of Riley's. She'd also asked – with much gesturing and helpful bits of mime – if she could borrow some washing powder so she could launder her clothes.

'Don't be daft,' I said. 'Let me have them and I'll put them through the machine for you.' But several visits to Google Translate and gentle argument later, I had to concede that she was not going to let me do that under any circumstances – that we had already done enough for her and she did not wish to be a burden. I didn't push it. Perhaps, I decided, thinking back to when I was 14, I would have baulked at a complete stranger washing my clothes as well.

There was also the business of her being independent. Having travelled so far, and taken care of herself for so long, she probably had a great deal of adjusting to do before she could truly settle into family life. I'd seen similar scenarios in children as young as seven or eight, particularly if they'd spent time in the care system. To strip them of their independence and privacy was to disable them even further – at least in the short term, when everything in their lives felt so out of their control. These were things that at least they *could* control.

Softly, softly then. I relinquished the washing gel and fabric conditioner. She did her clothes washing on Sunday morning, in the bath.

Happily, Adrianna's reticence didn't seem to extend to food, extreme hunger being a very powerful human state. And, boy, once she felt better and had a bit of colour in her cheeks, did she have an appetite. She sat down to Sunday lunch with an expression for which 'ravenous' was the only description.

'More potatoes?' I asked, grinning, having watching her devour all of hers within seconds.

She nodded, smiling at Tyler, who seemed mesmerised by the transformation. 'This good,' she said, accepting another scoopful. 'Your mammy make good food.'

Tyler blushed. And I knew it wasn't just because he was at the sharp end of her smile. He'd started calling us mum and dad a long time ago now, but there were still these little moments, when someone else referred to us as 'his mum and dad' when I knew it still had the power to bring him up short. Hard to explain, but entirely in a good way. It was almost as if he'd have to check with us – he glanced at me now – to be sure we didn't feel the need to explain that, actually, we weren't his *real* mum and dad. It was almost, though I didn't think it was even a conscious thing, as if he was testing us. That in all situations and with all people from here on in, mum and dad was what we were going to be. No qualifications. It truly mattered – it was a way of reconfirming his sense of security. It mattered to him – and in a whole host of different situations now – that we'd never felt the need to point it out. I could have hugged him.

'Well, I'm glad someone appreciates my cooking,' I said, laughing as I followed up with the dish of other vegetables. 'Thank you, Adrianna, I'm happy you like it.'

'I like it,' Adrianna repeated, nodding. '*Dziekuje di bardzo.*'

'That means thank you very much,' Tyler added, beaming.

Amazing how the small things so often are the big things, isn't it? A quiet family Sunday. Clean clothes. A good meal. Conversation. Laughter. All the basic needs met. And the change in Adrianna was profound.

I'd called Riley – still on a clothes mission, because my own stuff wouldn't fit our new visitor's slim frame – and wondered, when she said she'd pop round with all the grandkids that afternoon, if it might just be a little too much, too soon, for Adrianna. I couldn't have been more wrong. Though she was naturally a little shy with my extrovert daughter, she seemed to surf the wave of mayhem well. Almost painfully polite, and unfailingly well-mannered, she seemed perfectly at ease in a living room full of talkative people, where many 14-year-olds – it's such a gauche, self-conscious age – would have immediately scuttled to their rooms. What an enigma she was proving to be.

Particularly for Marley Mae, who, at almost three and, on home turf, was in her element. And wasted no time in monopolising Adrianna, either. Within 20 minutes of their arrival, she was already on her lap, completely mesmerised by her 'pretty princess' hair.

'She has a lot of Disney Princess dolls,' Riley told Adrianna, immediately taking my unspoken lead, and speaking in normal English, albeit slowly. 'Not sure which one she thinks you look like, but you have clearly struck a chord with her …'

'Disney,' said Adrianna, nodding. 'I know Disney.'

'Princess!' Marley Mae cooed. 'Pretty, pretty princess!'

Adrianna, in response, touched Marley Mae's hair – which was the usual muddle of dark, unkempt curls. She took to having her hair brushed and combed like a cat does to a dunking, i.e. not at all well.

'Princess too,' she told my granddaughter, laughing and kissing her head. 'You too. Disney Princess, named Mar-lee.'

Call me soppy – and you'd be right – but watching this small exchange, I felt a rush of emotion. It might be daft and unscientific, but my instinct has always been that anyone who displays such natural affection for a young, unrelated child must have a core of goodness in them. Easy to mock – and, of course, tragically, there are unhealthy variants of this scenario – but whatever else was true, I trusted my instinct in this. Our young Polish visitor was being fleshed out as a person before our eyes, and I was increasingly confounded by what I was seeing; this lovely young girl, seemingly all alone in the world, and interacting with Marley Mae with such natural affection. It made me feel sad to think that she must be craving attention of her own and had no one familiar around to give it to her. Or perhaps I was wrong – perhaps attention was exactly what Adrianna didn't need. Perhaps she was escaping something very bad and being with us was a means of avoiding whatever that something was.

'But you know what?' I said to John Fulshaw, when I called him first thing Monday morning. 'I don't think there's much point in the interpreter coming back just yet. Unless there's some protocol that requires you to get chapter and verse as a matter of urgency, I think we're better off letting her settle in a little more first.'

This wasn't just because my instinct was to first build on the success of our initial weekend together, and give Adrianna a chance to regain some equilibrium. It was also because she already had a keen interpreter in Tyler. And a much more amiable and pleasant one than had been provided by the council, for sure. Yes, this did mean she had learned his version of a number of words usually defined slightly differently, such as 'bad' and 'wicked', not to mention a couple of non-words, such as 'reem'. But that was fine – as a teenager, she'd need to familiarise herself with 'yoof' speak, even if it did mean she pronounced her

Sunday-night toasted sandwich 'standard', requiring our in-house interpreter to intervene.

'I was thinking much the same,' John said. 'I'm not sure Adrianna and Mr Kanski really hit it off, did they?'

'I'm not surprised,' I said. 'He wasn't the most likeable of men, was he? I got a strong sense that he was doing us some massive favour just by turning up. I don't know … I just didn't warm to him. Or his comment as he left, come to that. Of course she isn't telling us the truth! She's terrified of something, clearly, and grumpy old sods like him won't help tease her story out, will they?'

John laughed. 'Really? I'd never have guessed,' he said drolly. 'But that's fine. And actually, Casey, I'm inclined to agree with you about him. Oh, and I'm also going to hold off getting her a social worker for the moment, if it's all the same to you. It seems pointless to allocate her someone who can't understand a word she's saying, and I've a hunch I can put some feelers out and see if I can "buy" someone in from another area. Someone who speaks Polish, of course. In the meantime, can you manage? It doesn't sound like she's proving *too* challenging, and you never know – by this time next week, we might be moving her along anyway, mightn't we?'

I told him that was fine. 'Though, John, as I said, we're really in no rush. I think she *will* open up once she feels more settled.'

'You're a star,' he said. 'You all are. And – hey – learning a new language! Don't they reckon that's one of the best ways to stave off dementia? Anyway,' he added, 'while she's with you the service have also offered to do any translating you might need electronically. So if Adrianna is really struggling to get something across – or you are, for that matter – then they're happy for either of you to drop them an email and they'll translate it for you. It would be an improvement on what you'll manage online, for sure.'

That seemed a great idea – and definitely something I would try to encourage Adrianna to think about. But, in the meantime, I was more concerned that she get her health and strength back, and continue to make strides in terms of her learning to trust us, and to begin living a more normal life.

To which end, I decided, once I'd finished the call to John, that I'd take her out somewhere. She'd been stuck in the house for the best part of a week now, after all, and, with Tyler back in school, and just the two of us rattling around, I thought I'd take her out on a bit of a girly jolly, to buy some clothes for her, which were very badly needed, then perhaps pop in to Truly Scrumptious for some lunch. I knew Donna would be happy to see us and perhaps Chloe might be there too. And I was sure they'd hit it off.

And it seemed my idea would be a good one, because when Adrianna came down for her breakfast, her first utterance was 'Quiet, yes?' and her second a question: 'I go school, maybe? With Tyler? Sometime?'

It took me aback. After so long on the move – well, at least allegedly – I'd have imagined education might be the last thing currently on her mind. But, no, it seemed not. Quite the contrary.

'I'm not sure when, yet,' I said, as I prepared her a bowl of porridge. 'We need to wait till social services decide what's going to be best for you. Where you should stay. If you're determined that you're not going back home to Poland, that is.'

She shook her head, at least apparently understanding that last bit. 'No home,' she said. 'No *Polska*. I stay here in UK now.'

I nodded. 'Okay. And I am sure we'll find out soon. You must have missed so much school. Lots to catch up!'

I was all too aware how much I was modifying my language. How I was speaking so slowly, in clipped, simple sentences, enunciating so clearly, like something out of a comedy sketch about Brits abroad. But it seemed logical, because it at least gave her a chance to pick words out. Get the gist of it. Which I thought she probably did. She certainly seemed deep in thought as she sat and ate her breakfast.

How I'd have loved to have a real conversation with her. To know her concerns, what had happened to her, how I could help. How *we* could help. And not just us as a family. How we could help as a society. Or even if we *could* help – or should. I was so painfully ignorant of such political matters.

But I wasn't ignorant generally. I had never been that. This was a vulnerable child in need of support, and, as far as I was concerned, she could have come down from the moon. It made absolutely no difference to our duty of care to her.

Though I wasn't naïve, either. I knew not everyone would feel as I did. I didn't, however, expect to have that spelled out to me quite so starkly and so soon.

Adrianna proved easy to buy clothes for. Well, once we'd got past the business that I was determined to do just that – no arguments – and, via another series of comic hand gestures before we set off, making the point that she could not spend the foreseeable future with just one very elderly set of clothes.

We were soon, therefore, sorted. And Adrianna was kitted out with a small but decent wardrobe. Two distressed-looking T-shirts, bearing slogans – I had a suspicion she was a bit of a rock chick – plus a couple of hoodies and a nice pair of black skinny jeans. The very height of fashion, Riley had assured me. And once our haul was complete, including a selection of lingerie, socks and tights, we set off for our visit to my sister's café.

I'd hoped my niece Chloe might be working and was pleased to see she was. Though I doubted she had any more Polish than I did, there was a natural affinity between girls of similar ages, wherever they came from – one of the plus points of a global social media being that, culturally, they probably had more in common than they didn't.

And sure enough, once the complicated introductions were done with – and it is definitely tricky trying to establish 'sister' and 'niece' via the medium of flapping hands – Adrianna was coaxed into shyly showing Chloe our various purchases, while I went down the back with Donna to get some drinks for us.

We were late, in terms of the lunch crowd, so there was no problem getting a table; apart from a couple in the window and a young mum who was busy feeding her baby, we had the place pretty much to ourselves. The only other customers were a group of what I recognised as Donna's regulars: a trio of local ladies, all in their late sixties, who used the place weekly for a gossip and a catch-up. The kind of women you see everywhere. Cheerful. Innocuous.

Or so I'd thought. 'Hello, Casey, love,' the nearest of them said as I passed them. 'Long time no see.'

I agreed that it was.

'What you up to these days?' she continued. 'Still doing your fostering stuff? Donna told us you hung on to that boy.'

Leaving aside my irritation at the way she'd said 'that boy', I must have had some sort of instinct about her, because my first response – unspoken, obviously – was 'none of your bloody business'. Which was unlike me. So I smiled. 'Tyler,' I said instead. 'Indeed we did.'

I carried on past, but the woman half-turned her head. 'She one of yours too, then,' she said, nodding towards Adrianna, who was no more than a table away, with Chloe.

'Yes,' I said, 'Adrianna is staying with us for a while.'

It wasn't strictly necessary, but I slightly emphasised the word 'Adrianna', which was at least one step better than going 'Who's she? The cat's mother?', which was what it had been my impulse to say. I can't stand nosey parkers at the best of times, and she was a rude one, to boot.

Again, I carried on, plucking a menu card from the holder on the counter and scanning it, while Donna took the helm of her Italian whizz-bang coffee machine.

'Any good specials on today?' I asked her.

She began to reply – still with her back to me while she tapped and frothed and twiddled – but my attention was soon diverted by the word 'Polish'.

'Or Romanian or Lithuanian … There's so many of them now, aren't there? Can't bloody keep up with them. Basically the whole top half of the Eurovision Song Contest leader board,' one of the other women chortled.

I stopped scanning the menu. 'Makes no difference,' my earlier interrogator commented. 'They're all the same, aren't they? All come over here intent on stealing our bloody jobs. Do you know, Jean,' she told the woman sitting opposite her, 'my Simon got laid off from the crisp factory two months ago. Bloody eight years he'd worked there. Eight years! Then just like that,' she snapped her fingers to demonstrate, 'he was gone. Him and a fair few others, mind. Next thing we hear, only three weeks later they set a load of them bloody Eastern Europeans – that's what's they call them, or so our Simon says. I call them a bloody disgrace!'

They were talking to each other – not to me, not to Adrianna, but to each other. Which, ours being a free country, they had every right to do. But they were doing it *sotto voce*, clearly keen to be overheard.

So I decided to ignore them, even though I was seething inside.

Chloe, however, seemed to have other ideas. 'Er, excuse me?' she said. 'Hello? We're, like, just *here*?'

Donna and I both turned around. This was a turn-up. But the women appeared to ignore Chloe. 'And not content with stealing jobs and taking benefits,' the other one muttered, 'they start dumping their kids on social services now as well.'

The other women – definitely not ladies – muttered their agreement, one even prodding a finger at the open tabloid in front of her. 'Flipping disgrace, that's what it is …' An utterance that was followed by the evergreen, predictable 'and on tax-payers' money'. Donna and I exchanged looks.

'Jen, would you mind?' Donna said mildly, coming out from behind her counter. 'You know – entitled to your opinions and that, but … well …' She nodded towards the girls and made a small, almost apologetic, gesture.

'*Mum!*' Chloe said, anger flashing in her eyes.

I had some sympathy with my sister. After all, these were her regulars. Chloe, however, did not.

'Mum, they are being *outrageous*!' She glared at the three women. 'How can you be so rude!'

'We're only stating facts, love. To each *other*. Not you.'

'No you're not!' Chloe retorted. 'You're talking in stage whispers. On purpose! *Fortunately*, Adrianna doesn't speak much English, but *I* do, and those are completely outrageous things to say!'

Go my niece!, I thought. One of the A levels she was doing was Law. She'd make a cracking lawyer, I decided.

'Well, if the cap fits,' said the first woman. 'See, that's half the problem. *Why* doesn't she speak English? If these people refuse to integrate ...'

'Yet!' Chloe snapped at her. '*Yet* being the operative word. And, frankly, I can hardly believe such utter rudeness. Racist *rudeness*. Makes me ashamed to be British.'

Whatever Adrianna thought of all this – whether she had managed to get the gist of it – she was keeping her counsel, standing impassively at Chloe's side. For me, it was a blast. *Go that niece of mine!*, I thought again. Because the three women – who must have a combined age of pushing two hundred – were being seriously taken to task by an 18-year-old girl. I saw humiliation creeping into their expressions, even as they affected a look of indignant surprise.

'Well, I think we're about finished here, aren't we, Jen?' said the one who'd so far been the quietest. 'Soup was cold anyway ...' she huffed, rising and scraping back her chair.

'Good!' Chloe said, glancing quickly at her mother as she said so. 'So you'll probably want to eat elsewhere in future, won't you?'

If I'd been surprised before, I was open-mouthed at this. I glanced at Donna too – these customers were her livelihood, after all. But her expression was supportive and she made no move to intervene, even when the raised eyebrows on the woman called Jen seemed to suggest she might.

In the face of that, the three woman had no real choice but to bustle out, glaring at the other customers, whose expressions, hilariously, said it all. Indeed, as the bell on the door ding-a-linged to signal their departure, there was a necessarily small but heartfelt round of applause.

'Oh, God, I'm sorry, Mum,' Chloe said, immediately contrite and apologetic. 'I just – grrr – I couldn't help it. What racist old *bags*!'

'Lord, don't be,' Donna said, raising her hand and doing a thumbs-up to the other, now grinning customers.

'No, but I shouldn't have kicked off like that. They do have a right to their opinions. And I know some people *do* feel very strongly about immigration, because they are at the sharp end of things, aren't they? And there's so little *education*. People just don't know enough about the real facts. And this awful *rag* –' She stabbed an angry finger towards the now abandoned tabloid. 'But, God, they were just so *rude!*' She turned back to Adrianna. 'I mean, God, how would they like to be spoken about like that? Just bold as you like – with you standing right there in front of them!' Her face then broke into a smile. 'Sorry. Rant over. But I *am* sorry, Mum. I should have kept my cool a bit more.'

'I told you, *don't* be, love!' Donna said again. 'It's no loss to me, really. Yes, they come in every week, but it's only three bowls of soup, one pot of tea, no tip. So it's no loss. I was tired of their constant bitching anyway. Frees up a table for a better class of customer.'

I had no idea how much Adrianna understood, but she clearly appreciated her feisty new champion. '*Dzieki*,' she said. '*Thank* you. Thank you very much. You are so kind.'

57

'And I'm hungry,' I said. 'So, speaking of cold soup, can you heat some up? Proper, mind. Or I'm straight off to TripAdvisor.'

We eventually sat down to (hot, delicious) soup and cheese toasties with salad, and spent a pleasurable hour putting the world to rights. 'That's why this bloody country is in the state it's in,' Donna ranted, warming to the theme, 'through the ignorance and intolerance of bloody fools like them.'

Chloe grinned. Like mother, it now seemed, like daughter. She really would make an extremely good lawyer. As for Adrianna, perhaps more of a diplomat's role. 'But there are not so many like this,' she said, in her soft, halting English. 'Great Britain. Great people.' She smiled at us all. 'This is *true*.'

I squeezed her arm. I sincerely hoped it would prove to be.

Chapter 5

It's not up to me, obviously, to make such decisions, but the incident in Donna's café made me doubly sure that I should push no one about moving Adrianna on for now. Yes, in financial terms, she was indeed 'a burden on the state', but she was a tiny one in the scheme of things. And, in reality, left to fend for herself, she might be costing society even more. As a runaway on the streets the costs might not be so obvious, but they were there nevertheless, both in the short term and the long term, because kids on the streets were so often the victims of greater crimes – drug pushers, who'd get them hooked and then force them to commit petty crimes, usually theft, to create a steady income.

And even if they weren't sucked into drug use, they were still on course to become a greater drain on society; down the line, adrift and homeless, they'd often be unemployable, develop mental health problems and generally fail to become useful members of society.

And that was true of *all* kids who'd had a bad start in life. Most runaways were home-grown, after all – victims of a canker that was alive and well in our own country too. Which was why social services were always at full stretch.

'Blimey,' said Mike, when I ran my thoughts by him a couple of nights later. 'Are you planning to stand for parliament or something?'

I laughed, but there was a kernel of truth in his comment. Having listened to Chloe, and the passion with which she responded to knee-jerk racism, I had thought long and hard about exactly where Adrianna should fit in, and how I could – or should – justify our taking care of her.

Happily, when I spoke to John and suggested we didn't rush things with Adrianna, he agreed. 'And you're right,' he said. 'In terms of cost, she's in the best place at the moment. So if you're in no rush to move her on, I'm in no rush to try to do so. It sounds like she's settling in well, and, from what you tell me, in no rush to move on either.'

'Absolutely not,' I agreed. 'Though one thing – she'd love to go to school again. Is that feasible?'

'Complicated,' John said, 'but quite possible. The thing is that we have no idea of her educational background. She might not have gone to school for years as far as we know, and she isn't very forthcoming about all that, is she?'

'No, but she might be – if she thought she could go to school with Tyler, she might be. Plus there are Poles at his school she can make friends with, don't forget.'

'Good point,' John conceded. 'Tell you what, leave it with me. I'll speak with ELAC and see what they have to say.'

ELAC – yet another of the acronyms we bandied about – stood for the Education for Looked After Children team.

I'd had all sorts of dealings with ELAC over the years, and, unlike CAMHS, who often felt like the proverbial stone you wanted blood from (not their fault, they were the very personification of the word 'overstretched'), ELAC were always on top of their game, because schools often had spaces and everyone knew that a child in full-time education was in a markedly better place than one who was not. I mentally crossed my fingers. Her going to school might be key.

One thing was clear, though. That there was no need for an interpreter to return to us. Adrianna might only have basic English but with Tyler so keen to help her, and the extended family too (not least via the language of enthusiasm and encouragement), we could, I knew, get by just fine. And, I was sure – and I said as much to John – I would eventually get her to tell us more about her past. Not to mention, of course, that the only interpreter currently on offer was a grumpy old man. I'd rather muddle along as we were, thank you very much.

In the meantime, the present was looking good. Though Levi and Jackson were in school full time – as, obviously, was Tyler – there was always plenty going on with my two granddaughters. And Adrianna hadn't just struck a chord with Marley Mae, either. She loved being around little Dee Dee as well. Which, with our youngest grandchild soon to be one and on the very brink of walking, was a great help – extra pairs of watchful eyes being very much in demand.

My relationship with Lauren, always good, had moved to an even deeper closeness since the baby had been born, and, to my delight, she and Dee Dee visited often during the week, when Kieron was at work. Lauren herself, to help make ends meet, was still working flat out as a dance teacher, running classes several times a week for three- to ten-year-olds, but during the daytime I felt blessed that she was around so much, and I could watch my youngest grandchild grow and blossom.

Adrianna seemed to feel the same and, over the next couple of weeks, it was all about little-girl stuff. If it was raining we'd stay in and play endless games of shops and 'house', and when it was fine we'd wrap the girls up and often visit the park to play on the swings, and usually – Marley Mae's favourite thing, currently – to feed the park's many ducks and swans, not to mention the flocks of geese that had come to spend the winter with us from more northerly climes.

'To where it's warmer,' I heard Adrianna explain to Marley Mae as they threw bits of bread to the greedy web-footed hordes that ringed the boating lake. 'This is why they come to Britain.'

'Like you!' Marley Mae enthused.

'Like me. From far, far away. From the cold.'

'Cold,' Marley Mae parroted, stamping her feet in her little welly boots and going 'brrrr'.

Adrianna looked across the boating lake. Wistfully, I wondered? '*Very* cold where I come from,' she said. 'Much more cold than here. Freeze end of your nose,' she added, touching the tip of Marley Mae's.

But where? *Where* in the north? I filed the exchange away.

And it was through Marley Mae that we had another small breakthrough.

An enthusiastic if not entirely graceful young dancer, Marley Mae enjoyed the privilege of being able to start early in Lauren's once-a-week pre-schoolers dance class. It was for three- to five-year-olds really, and she wasn't three till April, but in a 'you scratch my back and I'll scratch yours' sisterly kind of arrangement, Lauren said she'd take her – she was desperate to go – and, in return, Riley was happy to take Dee Dee off Lauren's hands for a couple of hours a week so she could go shopping.

Marley Mae couldn't have been more excited. And, with her leotard and tutu having arrived when we got back to Lauren's after our latest park visit, she naturally had to try it on then and there. She looked like a real little ballerina after Adrianna scooped up her curls and fashioned them into a perfect bun on top of her head.

'Now you dance, Ad-i-annie!' she commanded, once she'd helped her wriggle into her outfit. 'We'll do twirling and splits,' she added helpfully. So it was that when Lauren returned from the kitchen, where she'd made us all drinks, it was to find the four of us – me and Dee Dee having been very much included – being taught a few basic ballet steps.

Lauren clocked this immediately. 'You can dance,' she said to Adrianna as she put the tray down in a sensible, out-of-the-way-of-dancing-toddlers place.

Adrianna blushed. 'I know ballet,' she said shyly.

'So I see,' Lauren said. 'You've danced a lot?'

A shadow seemed to cross Adrianna's face. And, remembering my first impressions about her bearing, I made a mental note of that, too.

She nodded. 'I did dance classes. Long time,' she admitted.

'Well, there's a turn-up,' Lauren said. 'And you know what,' she added, glancing at me, 'if Casey's okay with it, I could always use an extra pair of hands in the studio. If you fancy it, that is.'

Adrianna beamed. 'I fancy,' she said, nodding. Then she smiled down at Marley Mae, who was looking up to her adoringly. 'I love to teach the baby ballerinas.'

'Well, not so much baby ballerinas as baby elephants in tutus at the moment,' Lauren laughingly corrected. 'But I'm sure you'd enjoy it.' She glanced at me again. 'You could come along to tomorrow's class, if you'd like.'

Adrianna understood 'tomorrow'. She was beginning to get a grasp of the basics.

'Oh, yes,' she said. 'Thank you. Thank you so much. That would be sick.'

'Flipping Tyler!' Lauren and I said, together.

If I was chuffed that Lauren had made the suggestion that Adrianna go down and help her out with the little ones that Friday afternoon, Adrianna herself was euphoric.

Correction: appeared so. I didn't know her in any way well enough to be completely sure of that, but when Lauren came to pick her up, having dropped Dee Dee off at her other grandmother's (who usually looked after her while

Lauren ran her classes), the spring in her step was unmistakable. And when she returned home she was like a bottle of pop.

'Oh, Casey,' she enthused, once she was back inside and shrugging off her leather jacket, 'the tiny dancers were so beautiful. *So* graceful. Not like elephants. Like baby swans.'

She looked almost radiant, and it really warmed my heart. I was beginning to see these glimmers of happiness more and more now and, wherever she had come from, and whatever she'd endured, I felt this real surge of hope that, unlike so many kids I came across, there might well be a bright future in front of her; a light at the end of her mysterious, dark tunnel.

I made her hot chocolate. And as she seemed so light of heart and chatty, decided that this might be a good day to gently probe her. So I made myself one as well and sat down with her to drink it. Tyler was at his friend Denver's and we were going to eat late. So there was no hurry to start preparing tea.

I was particularly keen to know how and when she became the orphan she'd purported to be. She'd told both John and the interpreter that, and had refused to say more – something John assured me was actually quite a common lie they spun. That children, sent over by desperate parents, were told to deny the very existence of their mothers and fathers, in order that they wouldn't be sent straight back home.

I found this hard to fathom. Was anyone in Poland that desperate? It wasn't as if it was a third-world country, full of starving refugees.

It wasn't as if Adrianna fitted the profile of a starving refugee, either. 'So you have enjoyed helping with the dancing, then?' I said, as we both blew steam from our mugs.

She nodded. 'I love to dance,' she said. 'Always.'

Looking hard at my mug, I asked, 'Was your mother a dancer, Adrianna?'

I'd asked it as casually as I could. But perhaps not casually enough. Or too casually. She immediately looked wary.

'My dead mother,' she said slowly. 'She was a dancer as child.'

'And a good one?'

She nodded. 'She won compe – what is the word? Yes, competitions.'

'And did she teach you to dance?'

She glanced at me, assessing me. 'A little,' she said, nodding. 'But mostly classes.'

'Before she died?' Another nod. 'And afterwards?'

There was a pause, which soon became an uncomfortable silence.

In for a penny, I thought. 'It must have been so terrible for you,' I ventured. 'How old were you when your parents died, sweetheart?'

I had clearly overstepped the mark. 'I hate to talk about this,' she said, and her expression was apologetic. 'I am sad to, and –'

'Oh, sweetie, then I'm sorry,' I said. 'And we won't. I just wonder if, well, it might *help* you to talk. That's all.'

'It makes me so sad,' she said again.

Nothing for it then. Not for the moment. 'Enough then,' I said firmly. 'Now, tell me, d'you think we should see about getting you a leotard of your own?'

She immediately brightened. And then shook her head, grinning. 'No leotard for me. *No.* Only jogging pants. Definitely.'

'No leotard for me, either,' I said. 'As in for the rest of my natural life.'

Her brow creased and, to clarify, I grabbed the roll of flesh round my middle. 'As in no way do I plan on exhibiting this to all and sundry! Though, with your figure ...' I stopped and smiled at her, aware that I was gabbling on pointlessly. 'Anyway, enough of that, eh? So. When are you going next? To dance class,' I added, aware she might not understand me.

But she did. 'Monday,' she answered, draining her mug and getting up. 'So can I go do laundry now, please?'

I nodded, feeling stymied in my quest for more answers. She really did seem determined to keep her secrets locked away.

'Go ahead,' I said. 'But, really, as I keep telling you, there is no need. I do Tyler's, don't I? And it's no problem at *all* to do yours.'

She smiled at me. 'I like to. I am independent Polish girl!'

And, no question, that was exactly what she was. In fact, had it not been for the obvious barriers, I would have said that she was one of the most 'together' foster children we had ever cared for. Yes, it was still early days, but when you considered the circumstances of her coming into care, Adrianna didn't appear to have any obvious problems at all. Not behavioural, not emotional, not anything. Apart from when she'd been ill, not to mention scared in the beginning, she had been nothing but respectful and polite, as well as extremely helpful. Practically a model child, all told.

And yet, and yet … my fostering radar was still bleeping at me. There was something. Some *big* thing. I just wished I knew what.

'You and your flipping radar!' Mike chided later that night, when my tossing and turning were keeping him awake too. 'Can't you just let things be? Just be happy that life is simple, for a change. Why waste your energy now looking for problems in the future? Odds-on one'll be along soon enough.'

'Exactly!' I told him, as I grudgingly turned the light off.

'Exactly what?' he asked irritably.

'One'll be along soon enough. You know what they say,' I added. 'If something seems too good to be true, it usually is.'

'And?'

'And so *exactly*. That's exactly what I'm worried about!'

His answer was unprintable.

Chapter 6

I was having one of my periodic big cleans when I heard my mobile tootling at me. A full-on 'Casey-athon', prompted by the bright late-February sunshine, the prettily nodding daffodils in the pots on my back patio and the fact that the stars had aligned in such a way that I had the house all to myself for a change. Not to mention no grandmotherly duties to perform. I had the CD player blaring too, and was adding to my workout by attempting to twerk as I scrubbed the conservatory floor, there being no risk of anyone seeing me.

And it was a happy twerk, as it had proved to be a positive couple of weeks, during which Adrianna had really seemed to blossom. There was no doubt that Lauren's interest in her had made a massive difference. And, though I definitely had no intention of going into politics, had you given me a soap box I'd have clambered upon it instantly to point out to the likes of some of my sister Donna's *former* customers that humans are good in the vast majority of cases – good, and responsive to positive interventions, such as being given the chance to make some sort of contribution, and having their skills and propensity for work appreciated.

I wasn't a naïve, fanciful idiot and I knew politics were complex, but I really wanted to hold Adrianna up as a kind of poster girl, almost, to prove the power of trying to always see the best, rather than the worst, in our fellow *Homo sapiens*. Luckily for the world there were no soap boxes within reach.

I was also tickled, and very touched, by Adrianna's relationship with Tyler, whom I feared (because Adrianna was still likely to be but a temporary fixture) was as besotted by her as was Marley Mae.

And to an extent that even Mike and I possibly hadn't quite appreciated, evidenced by the fact that, only a couple of days previously, he'd returned from an after-school sortie to the shops and presented Adrianna with a gift.

She'd looked stunned, slightly embarrassed and, very soon, extremely tearful, as she opened the bag, which contained a paperback book.

'It's *Lord of the Flies*,' he'd explained as she ran her hand over the cover. 'I know it's not your birthday or anything,' he clarified. 'Well, not as far as we know, anyway. I just thought I'd give it to you as a way of saying sorry. For having made you learn all my silly words.'

'Oh, Tyler,' I couldn't help but say, clapping my hands together happily. 'What an incredibly thoughtful boy you are.'

His blush, always threatening, now deepened percepti-
bly. 'It's one of the first proper books I ever read,' he said
to Adrianna, glancing briefly at me and Mike. 'Casey gave
it me,' he explained. 'D'you remember?' he said to me.
'Remember you trying to get me to read it when I first
came? And I was, like, sorry, but I don't read books? It's
still up in my bedroom,' he added to Adrianna. 'But I
thought you'd want to have your own copy. To keep. It's
brilliant. You'll like it. And it'll help with your English,
too.'

Adrianna had been speechless. Had sobbed her thanks
rather than said them. And had started reading the book
right away.

It was a while before the sound of my phone filtered
through to me past the warbling of my disco classics compi-
lation – 'Rock the Boat', currently – and it had stopped and
restarted by the time I'd downed tools, stripped my
Marigolds and remembered where the phone was. Which
turned out not to be in my handbag over the banister, as I'd
thought, but on its charger in the kitchen, having been
forgotten in my handbag the previous evening and run out
of juice. No wonder that my children so often despaired of
me.

'Ah, so you *are* there,' came Lauren's voice – for it was
her name on the phone display. 'It's me.' She sounded
stressed. 'Are you driving?'

'No,' I told her, immediately thinking of Dee Dee round
at her other gran's. 'I'm at home. What's wrong?'

'It's Adrianna. She's collapsed. The paramedics are examining her now, and –'

'Adrianna? *Paramedics*?' I switched immediately into stressed mode myself. 'God, what's happened?'

'I'm not sure. *They're* not sure. She just – well – she just keeled over. She'd been looking a bit green, saying she was feeling a little hot and couldn't seem to catch her breath, and, well, she just kind of folded up while she was showing the girls some bar stuff. Honestly, she was lucky she was right by the pile of floor mats. It was just, like, "whump" – she went down like a ton of bricks.'

'You mean fainted?'

'That's what we thought. But then we couldn't bring her round. Which was frightening, to say the least.'

'God, I'll bet –'

'Which was why I called the ambulance. They've just arrived.'

'Oh, lord,' I said, my mind whirring. Had she seemed ill earlier? No, she hadn't. Pale, of course, but she seemed always to be, and we were used to that now. 'So is she still out for the –'

'It's okay,' Lauren reassured me quickly. 'She's conscious again now. But they want to take her to hospital to examine her properly. She's not quite with it,' Lauren explained. 'I'm not sure she's herself. She's struggling to make herself understood by the paramedics, which makes it hard for them to assess her, and, what with the girls all going mental, and everything else –'

'Oh, lord,' I said again. 'Poor you. So shall I come straight down there?'

'No, I was thinking that probably wouldn't work. I'm going to go in the ambulance with her, so … could you maybe drive down and meet us at the hospital?'

'You sure? It won't take me long to get to you. What about the girls?' Some 15 of them – eight- to ten-year-olds, if I remembered rightly. A bit of a handful.

'It's okay. There's no problem there. Debbie's here today as well. She'll stay here till all the girls are collected so I can go with Adrianna. Which I have to. Honestly, she's in *such* a state, Casey … I can't let her go in the ambulance on her own. Mind you, I've got to get back to collect Dee from my mum's, because – oh, yes … hang on a tick, Casey …'

Debbie was Lauren's friend, who came sometimes and played the elderly piano. Thank goodness for that, at least, I thought. I wondered what on earth could be wrong with Adrianna. Since her initial virus she'd seemed fine, by and large. No, not perfect, but I'd begun to put that down to a general long-term lack of nourishment. If she'd been sleeping rough it was odds-on she'd been eating appallingly, and it would take time for her body to build itself back up. But you never knew, did you? She might be anaemic, for example. Girls could be, at her age, if they suffered heavy periods. That fitted with her paleness, and the way she'd romped through my 'girl' supplies soon after arriving. And anaemia could definitely cause her to pass out … And the timing was right. She'd been with us a month …

But I knew it was pointless to speculate. The most important thing was to get there, so I tugged at the strings on my cleaning apron while Lauren finished speaking to whoever she was talking to. I heard the rumble of a male voice, presumably one of the paramedics. And was that Adrianna's voice I could hear in the background? Wailing?

'Okay,' Lauren said again. 'Casey, I've got to go. Meet you there? In A&E, I imagine … I'm so sorry …'

'No, no. Of course, love,' I reassured her. 'I'm on my way.'

I pressed the end button with an unexpected feeling. Not of foreboding – even though I couldn't quite say why I didn't feel that. No, it was more one of expectation finally fulfilled – of having been waiting for this day to dawn all along. Now perhaps we'd finally get some answers.

I was in the car minutes later, but only making ten-mile-an-hour progress, having been caught up in the traffic bulge on the road out to the hospital. It was the last of the school run mingling with the beginnings of the rush hour, the sun dipping down now and winking off the rows of cars.

And, as I expected, it was a full 40 minutes before I turned into the hospital grounds, now mostly in shadow, as the watery late-winter sun was almost gone. Happily, though, the visitor car park was beginning to empty, and, having rummaged for the requisite king's ransom for the privilege, I was soon parked up and hurrying across to Accident and Emergency.

My sense of inevitability was by now even stronger. I had no idea *what* had happened, but wasn't remotely surprised that *something* had. It could be nothing, of course – and I sincerely hoped so, obviously – but, on the other hand, for all that we'd all commented on the improvement since that first week, Adrianna had never really seemed completely well since she'd come to us – not well in the accepted 'rude health' kind of way. I wondered again if she was seriously anaemic. Or – another thought I'd had simmering on a back burner – perhaps anorexic, or bulimic, and just extremely good at hiding it. She was still painfully thin, despite the huge appetite we'd all remarked upon, and so private in her habits that it was impossible to know.

Or perhaps – and more prosaically – she was simply suffering from some kind of post-viral syndrome. Though I'd never had personal experience of it, I knew things like glandular fever could linger for weeks, even months. Then there was ME – myalgic encephalomyelitis. Which was something you didn't really hear much about anymore, but was presumably still diagnosed.

And there was so little of Adrianna, physically, to fight anything off. And we still knew hardly anything of the circumstances that had preceded her coming to us. How did we know she wasn't suffering from some long-standing illness? She might be immune-compromised. Have Addison's disease (something we'd come across in another child). Or be an as yet undiagnosed diabetic.

There was a whole host of medical possibilities, clearly. And, being no doctor, I should stop trying to second-guess the one who was (hopefully) soon going to be attending her. Still, I thought, as the Casualty doors hissed and parted to admit me, at least now there was no question of her avoiding being properly examined by one. Male or female, whether she liked it or not. Despite my stresses about what might be ailing the girl, I had this overriding feeling that I was about to get to the bottom of something, which of course I probably was, but it was more than that, and it gave me butterflies in my tummy as I rushed ahead.

The waiting room was half full, and a quick scan revealed no sign of Lauren, whom I presumed was with Adrianna in a side room or cubicle. It was just the usual mix of late-afternoon Accident and Emergency patients. A couple of pensioners, sitting patiently. A man hopping along on crutches. A young mum jiggling a grizzling baby on her lap. Another mum, trying to calm a six- or seven-year-old boy with some sort of leg wound, while simultaneously trying to quieten what was obviously a younger sibling – fresh out of school, still full of energy, and running amok in the aisles.

Back in the day I remembered there being a pretty well-stocked play area. But, along with magazines and picture books, health and safety had obviously long since put paid to that – and in doing so, I reflected, watching the man on crutches dodging the pink-cheeked little boy, creating all sorts of other health and safety issues in its place.

There were two people in front of me in the queue for the receptionist, so I used the time to text Mike and let him know where I was, having rushed out of the house without thinking to leave a note. At least I didn't need to worry about Tyler. He was having tea over at Denver's and

Mike was collecting him on his way home from work, but knowing A&E as I did (and I'd certainly been a regular attendee in my time), there was a fighting chance that once Adrianna had been booked in and triaged there would still be a lengthy wait for treatment. Well, unless she had something seriously wrong with her, of course. I pressed 'send' on the message – which, as I was in a notoriously signal-challenged place, failed to go – and could only hope not.

And it seemed not. At least, as far as the receptionist knew. 'She's being seen now,' she explained, once I'd told her who I was. 'So if you'd like to take a seat, I'm sure there'll be some more news soon.'

'I can't go to her?'

'Well, you *could*, but I don't know where she is currently. If you'll let me see to this gentleman' – she nodded to a man who was now standing behind me – 'I'll try to find out for you.'

With nothing for it but to wait, I decided against a seat in the waiting room itself, preferring to head off to where I knew there was a bank of vending machines and, crucially, a better mobile-phone signal.

And it seemed I wasn't the only one who'd had the same idea. I'd no sooner sent the message to Mike than I saw Lauren in the distance, approaching from the far end of the long corridor that led to the main building. She waved when she saw me and speeded up.

'She's okay,' she said as soon as she reached me, in answer to my as yet unspoken question. 'But they've admitted her.

To one of the medical wards. Number 7.' She tapped her temple. 'Remembered to make a mental note of it. Though there's probably no point in you going up there just yet, because I think they're about to take her down for an ultrasound scan and, depending on that, I think she might be going to surgery. Oh, and she's got to have a blood transfusion, which they'll do at the same time.'

'A *blood transfusion*?'

Lauren nodded. But she was glancing at her phone, checking the time. She looked distracted about something. 'Er, yes … sorry, look – I really need to call my grandma before I do anything else,' she said. 'Mum had to drop the baby round to her, because she had a tooth drilled and was feeling really icky. And she'll be wondering where on earth I've got to, bless her. Bloody hospitals – they're like black holes, aren't they?'

'Just go, love,' I urged. 'Don't worry. You don't need to stay now. You get off. I'll sort all this out.'

Lauren shook her head. 'No, no – just let me do this –' She was texting with her thumbs while she was speaking, a skill I had not as yet been able to acquire – and probably never would.

'No really, just *go*,' I said again, thinking of her poor gran. She was at least in her late sixties and not the nimblest on her feet.

Lauren shook her head again as she finished composing her text. 'There. That's that done. Don't worry. Kieron will call her now. And listen, before I go, I need to tell you something.'

It was only now that I realised she had something else pressing on her mind. 'Tell me what?'

'Something you are *not* going to believe, trust me.'

Which would have worried me, were it not for the fact that I could read Lauren's expression. Which was shocked, yes. But not accompanied by any signs of distress. So, what could it be then?

'Go on, then,' I said. 'Try me.'

'You might want to sit down first …' she said, taking my arm and drawing me to the side of the corridor, so that a gaggle of medics could pass by.

'Sit *down*? Now you're worrying me. Go on. What? What's so shocking?'

'You're never going to believe this. Adrianna isn't 14 at all. She's 16 –'

'*Sixteen*?' There was clearly more to come than this. 'Sixteen? *Really*? And?'

'And she collapsed because she's had some sort of birth complication.'

I almost spluttered. '*Birth* complication? *How*?' The words came out of my astonished outbreath.

'*Exactly*. That's what I thought. But it's true, Casey. She's had a *baby*! And, by all accounts, literally just the day before she came to you!'

Chapter 7

I gawped at Lauren, stunned. I think my mouth was probably hanging open. But then, after hovering in front of my mind's eye for a few seconds, each piece of the jigsaw began settling neatly into place.

Her laundry. I almost laughed out loud at my own stupidity – not to mention my complete naïvety – in not putting two and two together. Not that I was *that* daft – I had a 14-year-old female staying in the house. So making her aware of the location of all the feminine supplies she might need had been one of the first things I'd done. That was taken as read, and we didn't discuss the matter further. Why on earth (*how* on earth) would we? Jeepers – I'd even reflected on it half an hour back, hadn't I? Had even wondered about the possibility that she might be anaemic as a result of having heavy periods. Why never *this*?

But the washing. What an idiot. The whole issue around the washing. All these weeks and one thing had been an absolute constant; that Adrianna wouldn't, under any circumstances, allow me to do her washing. Not so much as a sock. And not even her bedding, which, strictly speaking, was *our* bedding. But which she absolutely would not let me get even slightly involved with, stripping it and changing it and washing it herself – sometimes, it seemed, almost by stealth. Definitely, more often than not, when she was alone in the house. I'd come back to find it laundered, ironed and back in its place. As if she were a little domestic fairy.

Which was fine, or so I'd thought, in as much as I did think – independence, thought I. Not wanting to be a burden, thought I. Some cultural detail that I didn't understand, thought I. What an enormous great klutz I had been. It had been right there under my nose. Our 'independent Polish girl' had been all of that, with knobs on. She'd been recovering from childbirth, for goodness' sake!

The jigsaw complete, I pulled my lower jaw back up again.

'Okayyy,' I said to Lauren. 'Just updating the database. So. Sixteen.'

'So they say.'

'They?'

'There's a nurse who speaks Polish.'

'Blimey, that was lucky.'

'Apparently not,' she said. 'There are several here. The doctor was joking with me, actually – says it's like a regular United Nations. Says at the last count they've got something like 20 languages covered. Anyway, yes. She's the sister on the medical ward Adrianna's been put on. And they sent for her. She came down and joined us in A&E when we first arrived.'

'And Adrianna really gave birth just the day before coming to us? She actually told them that?'

Lauren nodded. 'Apparently so. That's why she ended up going to social services. Anyway, listen. I told her – the nurse, that is – you know, what the situation is, and everything. And who you are, and so on. Hope that's okay. And I told her you were on your way. So she's expecting you. She's really nice. And she's on a late, too. She says she'll fill you in on as much as she can …'

Lauren glanced at her phone again. 'God, sorry, love,' I said. 'Go on. Skedaddle. Get yourself home to the baby.'

The baby. The thought hit me, but it was too late to call Lauren back.

What had happened to Adrianna's? I felt cold.

After explaining to the receptionist – who seemed to have forgotten I was there anyway – that I no longer needed her help, I walked slowly out of the double glass doors to get some air before going to Ward 7.

Since I had a signal – and the hospital had recently ended its decade-long cold war on the dangerous, life-threatening forces previously deemed to be living inside mobiles – I thought I would call Mike as well.

'You know what?' he said, once I'd gabbled through everything and bemoaned the fact that my fostering antennae must have been tuned to the wrong channel. 'She is one dark horse, that one. I would *never* have suspected that. *Sixteen?*'

'Sixteen.'

'And the day before?'

'The day before. Beggars belief, doesn't it? I mean, you'd never have guessed, would you? I mean, there's nothing *of* her, for one thing – how on earth didn't we see? I mean – not to be too graphic – but her boobs and her stomach? Christ – after Riley I felt like a whopping great blancmange! It took weeks for me to get back some sort of shape. How didn't we *see*, Mike? I just keep coming back to that. I feel terrible. I should have *seen* …'

'Oh, for goodness' sake, Case – because she made sure you *couldn't*. That was why.'

And I realised that he was right. There was no way we were going to know, because she made damn sure we couldn't. Because it mattered that much to her that we didn't know anything about it. But *why*?

Stop bloody speculating, my sensible inner voice said. *Go and find out, you stupid woman.* And she was right. That was exactly what I must do. 'Anyway,' I said to Mike. 'I'm heading up there now and I don't know how long I'll be, because there's talk of an operation. They're fairly sure they'd be operating. And doing a blood transfusion, too. So I'm not sure about tea. Shall we –'

'Fish and chips,' he finished for me. 'Seeing as it's Friday. Though you'll need some things for her, won't you? Can't imagine they'll let her home tonight, can you? Not if she's – *God*, all this time, and we had no flipping *idea*!'

'Tell me about it,' I said. 'I can't quite take it in. I just –'

'What happened to it,' Mike interrupted, his voice low. 'That's the thing, isn't it? What's she *done* with it?'

'Exactly,' I said. 'God, Mike. D'you think she dumped it somewhere and ran away? D'you think that's why she's been so tight-lipped about everything? Because she thinks she'll go to prison for it? God –' I stopped, it all suddenly beginning to make perfect sense.

'What?'

'What if it was stillborn or something? Or what if she …' I couldn't quite bring myself to say it. Desperate young girl. Far from home. Penniless and terrified …

'Stop bloody whatting,' Mike commanded. 'Go and flipping find *out*.'

He was right. I needed to skedaddle myself, and fast.

I went back inside to see a small knot of people now by the vending machine. And a marked increase in human traffic on the main corridor. The main artery, I thought, pleased with having thought of the analogy. A hospital really was a lot like the human body; a complex dynamic system that all fitted together – almost like a living, breathing thing.

And one in hyper-drive, I thought as I joined the river of people and wound my complicated way from Accident and Emergency on the ground floor to the medical ward Lauren had directed me to on the fourth – a journey that took a good ten or fifteen minutes.

Hospitals have their own rush hours, and once again I had found it. The office staff leaving, the outpatient clinics closing, the various ward staff and ancillary workers doing change-overs and patient transfers, plus – as the various aromas on my journey confirmed – the massive operation that was feeding tea to the presumably several hundred inpatients. A big university hospital such as ours was really a whole community in itself. All human life really was represented here.

I wasted no time in speculating about the circumstances of Adrianna's labour – well, except to be clear that it probably hadn't taken place in any hospital, because there was no way in the world they'd have discharged her. Unless she'd run away, of course. Which I had to concede could have happened if she'd been determined.

But once again, it was pointless to speculate. No, I was on a mission now; to find the nurse to whom Adrianna had spoken when she'd first arrived here, and, while Adrianna was safely out of the way having her scan, to try to establish as many details as I could.

And, happily, I found the nurse in question almost right away. The nurses' station was at the entrance to the ward and, like nursing stations everywhere, was the beating heart of their patch of the hospital. There was a big white wipe-clean back board that held details of patients and their locations, framed by a dense border of overlapping thank-you cards. There was a high counter, behind which two nurses currently sat surrounded by the usual array of paperwork. As in hospitals and in teaching and fostering, I mused. The usual, tedious, endless slews of paperwork.

And I spotted her without a moment's hesitation, by virtue of the surname on her badge. She was a tall woman, pale skinned and long limbed and fair – and definitely not at all Polish-looking. Not in my admittedly limited experience, anyway. She was standing beside the seated nurses, her hand cradling a mug, and when she looked at me I realised she'd recognised me too. I smiled, imagining what Lauren might have said to her. Five foot nothing. Long black hair. There was little else needed, was there?

Obviously not. 'Ah, you must be Mrs Watson,' she said, smiling back. 'Adrianna's foster mum?'

I nodded. 'That's me.'

'She's down having a scan at the moment,' she went on. 'So –'

I nodded again. 'I know.'

'Ah, your daughter-in-law found you then,' she said. There wasn't so much as a trace of a Polish accent, which surprised me.

'Yes she did, and I'd love a chance to chat to you, if you can spare the time. Lauren said she explained? That we're fostering Adrianna temporarily? And, well, as you can imagine, this has all come as something of a shock. And what with the language barrier, you can imagine it's such a *huge* help that she's been able to talk to you. We had an interpreter round early on, but Adrianna really didn't take to him, and with none of us speaking any Polish ...'

She drained her mug and nodded. 'Yes, of course I can. Well, what little I know so far, at any rate. Come into the day room,' she said, coming round from the back of the station. 'It's this way.'

Sister Skaja – for that was her name – didn't look Polish, it turned out, because she wasn't. She was English. From somewhere in Kent. She spoke Polish because she had been married to a Polish man for a very long time. And had made a real effort at it too, she explained, because they wanted their children, all now grown-up, to be bilingual. So it was both my and Adrianna's lucky day.

Sister Skaja explained that Adrianna would indeed be kept in overnight. Till early next week, in all probability. Possibly longer. 'She is seriously anaemic,' she explained. 'Probably due to chronic blood loss following the birth. Which is probably the result of birth trauma, and there being retained products. Which could obviously lead to peritonitis, if it hasn't already, so, once she's had her scan, I imagine they'll call the on-call gynae surgeon in because they'll have to deal with that as a matter of urgency.'

'So it's quite serious?' I said, feeling a fresh wave of guilt, remembering the need for the transfusion. How the heck hadn't we known about all this?

Sister Skaja placed a hand over mine. 'She'll be *fine*,' she reassured me. Yes, it's urgent that it's done, but it's usually a routine procedure. Though we'll obviously have to keep her in for a bit, as she'll need IV antibiotics. Then, all being well, she will be right as rain. She's young and fit, of course, which helps enormously, obviously.'

'She must be,' I said. 'So she did give birth alone, then? Hence the business of –'

'Oh, yes. Definitely. No question. Well, in terms of there being no medical or nursing support on hand.'

'She told you that?'

'She didn't have to.'

'And the baby. What about the baby?'

'I'm afraid I can't help you there. She'd already got herself in such a state, bless her, and became almost hysterical pretty much as soon as I asked her about the baby. Sobbing and wailing – absolutely terrified she was going to die.'

'But you managed to get something out of her.'

Sister Skaja nodded. 'Oh, yes, a few things, as your daughter probably already told you. Only the bare bones as yet. That she's 16 – that was pretty much the first thing she told me. I think she was worried that if she lied about it she'd be in trouble. Particularly when she admitted what she thought was probably wrong with her. So, yes, 16. And that she ran away from home a couple of years back.'

'From home?'

'That's what she said.'

'Not from *a* home? Like a children's home?'

She shook her head. 'No, those were her exact words – that she'd run away from home two years ago ...'

From *home*. So there *was* a home. And presumably living, breathing parents. Or parent singular. 'So when she was 14.

Oh, God love her … What else? Did she tell you why she ran away?'

'To escape a stepfather – she came back to that – him – a couple of times. That, and that she must not be sent back there.'

'What about the mother?'

She nodded again. 'Yup, she's definitely got one of those. Well, if you could call her that. By all accounts it was the mother who told her to sling her hook.'

'So they chucked her out?' So far, I thought, so bloody wretched.

'I'm not clear, to be honest. She was rambling a little. Either way, it seemed clear there was no "home" as such to return to.'

I could feel my shoulders sagging. Another thing that was universal. I sighed. 'Is there a real dad, do you know?'

'Dead. Quite a while back. That was all I managed to get out of her about him.'

'And the stepdad?' I had a sudden thought. A grim one. One I wished hadn't struck me quite so readily. And then another one, hot on the heels of it. Two years. Well, in theory. And who knew what had happened since then. 'There's no way the baby is his, is there?'

Sister Skaja shook her head. 'No. That was my thought too, as it happens. But no. Nothing like that. She's been in the UK for over a year now.'

I felt my brows lift. 'A year? *Really?*'

'Apparently so.'

'Doing what? Living where? Did she say?'

'No, she didn't. She said she'd been moving around a lot in Poland, and came over with a man she'd met through a girl she knew.'

'A boyfriend? The father?'

'Not sure. She was gabbling on about him lying to her. How there was supposed to be a job with his family – in some sort of shop. But naturally, there wasn't. And a home for her, and all the usual bloody enticements …'

She sounded like she knew what they were, too. 'None of which materialised?' I had another thought. 'You said "naturally". Did she tell you something else?'

Sister Skaja sighed and checked her fob watch. 'No. That was pretty much all of it. For now, anyway.' She then stood up, so I did too. She obviously had to get back to the ward. And I couldn't keep interrogating her for ever. 'Well, except that she was living with some other girls. All Polish, like her,' she added. She turned and looked at me through narrowed eyes as she pulled open the dayroom door. 'You do know where this is probably going, don't you?'

I didn't. I said so. I told her I was still too busy trying to take everything else in. 'So what do you think *is* going on, then?' I asked her.

'They'll all be runaways,' she said, as I followed her back to the nurses' station. 'Pound to a penny they will be. All trafficked.' She paused. 'Sickening, isn't it? God, there aren't words to cover it. Scum of the bloody earth.' She turned around again, shaking her head sadly. 'That's what'll have happened. She'll have been trafficked, for sure. Well, that's my reading of things, anyway. He'll – or rather they, because I've no doubt there's probably a gang of them – they'll have been working the lot of them as prostitutes.'

'And the baby ...'

It was more of a statement than a question. Sister Skaja answered it anyway.

'Collateral damage. Pound to a penny. Poor girl.'

Chapter 8

So there it was. The whole mystery of Adrianna's background laid bare. The whole reason for that haunted, frightened look in her eyes. The whole reason, I didn't doubt, why she'd not let the doctor near her. Why she'd reveal nothing, say nothing, admit nothing about her past. There it was. All come back, now, to haunt her. But after what? After she'd hoped it would simply all go away? Was that what this was about? That she'd hoped to reinvent herself somehow? As a 14-year-old, washed up in a faraway country? To begin again, go to school, start completely afresh? To erase the past, and the baby that went with it? As a version of the truth, I had to concede that it certainly had legs.

But that was all it was – a version. I still had no idea what she'd been thinking. Much less what she was thinking right this minute, now her untruths had been exposed. And there was still, clearly, much more to know.

Yes, Adrianna had admitted to having had a baby, but where *was* that baby? From the snatches of information

Sister Skaja had been able to extract from her, that little detail was still up for grabs. She'd been distressed, sister Skaja had reminded me as I left. And she had also been given a powerful sedative in the ambulance, so was drifting, incoherent and gabbling to boot. And what she *had* apparently said – that she had 'lost it' – could mean anything. Well, in reality, more than likely one of just three things – that it had died naturally, or she'd abandoned it, or that someone else was now taking care of it.

In my view, in any case, and it was one I was keen to stick to, because Sister Skaja's view – that, just possibly, there was another scenario up for grabs – was one I couldn't bring myself to consider. Not that she had any evidence for it. She'd been extremely keen to stress that. But she'd also, as she'd put it, 'been around the block a few times' and knew more than she wished she did 'about girls who get trafficked'. And she didn't think it inconceivable that Adrianna, desperate, alone and all too aware of her baby's grim paternity, could have made the decision to take its life.

No, not that. I couldn't see it. Or, more accurately, wouldn't. I too had 'been around the block', and knew a great deal more than I wished to, but I simply didn't think she'd be capable.

'Who am I kidding, though?' I asked Mike, once I'd gone back down to the main hospital concourse and phoned him again. 'We hardly know her. Yes, we think we do, but how much do we really know about her? She could be capable of anything, couldn't she? With everything that's happened to her, God only knows where her head is. Anyway, I'm going to stay here till she's back from her scan, because I'm told I'll probably get a chance to see her before she's taken to surgery. Which I think I must – don't you? Just to let her know we're here for her. See if there's anything she'd like me to bring in.'

Like me, Mike was shocked, but at the same time he wasn't. A contradiction in terms, perhaps, but true nonetheless. Much as it was shocking to hear about the birth of the baby, it was also true that children came into the care system for one reason, pretty much – because their childhoods thus far had been some kind of train-wreck, their care non-existent, their mental state fragile, their 'back-story' invariably the same miserable cocktail of neglect and/or abandonment and/or cruelty and/or abuse.

And, by the sound of it, when writing up my log on Adrianna later, I could probably just put 'all of the above'.

'Why don't I just bring some things up now?' Mike said. 'Save you going back and forth, won't it? Tyler's happy to wait for tea, and it won't take me long.'

'Go on, then,' I said, grateful. 'You know what to bring. Night things. The usual toiletries. Oh, and why don't you bring her book in for her too? The one Tyler bought her? If she's going to be in for a few days, she'll probably be glad of it …'

There was a catch in my throat; saying that, I actually felt tearful. But if he noticed, Mike politely refrained from ribbing me about it. Instead, he noted down what was needed and promised he'd be up within the hour. So, having rung off and grabbed myself a super-heated hospital vending-machine 'coffee', I found a seat in a quiet corner and sat down to call John.

He was as unsurprised as Mike, perhaps even less so. 'Well, that all sounds pretty much the sort of thing we expected,' he commented. 'Though her being 16 makes a bit of a difference to how we proceed, obviously. I'll have to get in touch with my line manager and see where we need to go from here. The poor kid. What's she been *doing* all this time? Where's she been living since she got away? *When* did she get away, for that matter? I can't quite see them offering her up for business when she was heavily pregnant. Though …' He paused. 'No, I think I'll just unthink that thought.'

I had my own thought. 'D'you think he – they – whoever – will have been looking for her?'

'Maybe, but maybe not. If this is what I think it is, i.e. trafficking, then a missing girl or an escapee could be simply seen as collateral damage. On the other hand, if she was valuable to them, then perhaps they may have someone on the lookout for her. She'd be able to identify them, wouldn't she?'

'Except *would* she do that? I've always had the impression she wants to disappear off the radar. Lying about her age. Coming so far. Keeping quiet about the baby. Which does make sense, if she's been terrified of being arrested, doesn't it? But it was lucky, then, wasn't it? That she got transferred to here.'

'Not necessarily. She might have travelled *from* here – or somewhere near here – to put distance between them, mightn't she? She might, in fact, have been brought back to where she *least* wants to be.'

'I hadn't thought of that. God, we so need her to tell us everything, don't we?'

'That we do,' said John. 'So I'll put a call in. See if we can get the interpreter pencilled in again sooner rather than later. We'll obviously need to have a more formal discussion with Adrianna now, and –'

I had another thought. 'Is there anyone else? You know, in terms of interpreters? I know beggars can't be choosers, but I just feel she'll open up more if it's a woman she's speaking to. Particularly now we know what we know, don't you think? Because if it's all true, I can see why she'd be wary ...'

'Good point,' John said. 'Much as I hate to say it, you might be right. Particularly if she's anxious about someone finding out where she is. Leave it with me and I'll see what I can do. And if anything else comes up, don't worry about calling me over the weekend, will you? I've got absolutely nothing in the social diary for a change. The wife's obviously slipping ...'

He chuckled. I did too, as I agreed that she must be. It was a pertinent reminder that normal life trundled on. 'Seriously,' he finished. 'We'll get all this sorted. And no all-night vigils, you hear? I know what you're like.'

Which couldn't have been truer, because it had already crossed my mind that if Adrianna did go down to surgery, which seemed likely, she'd presumably come round, late this evening, in a strange hospital bed, with no familiar face to reassure her. So just perhaps …

I ticked myself off as I binned my empty coffee cup. There was no way I could sleep on a camp bed in a parents' room. For one thing (I ticked items off my fingers as I walked) it would be late, she'd be sedated, there would be nothing I could do for her, and for another, she wasn't on a ward with a parents' room. Beds were short. She was on an adult medical ward. And for another – and this was the clincher, I decided – there was no way in the world Mike would let me.

That established, at least provisionally – much would depend on how she was – I made my way up to the ward. A good half hour had passed now, so I assumed she'd have had her scan done, and this was confirmed when I noted the nurses' station board, which had obviously been updated. Adrianna – just Adrianna still; no surname given – was apparently the patient in bed six.

Sister Skaja was now seated at the nurses' station, writing. She looked up and smiled when she saw me. I sensed an ally, and felt reassured that she was on a late shift.

'How is she?' I asked her.

'As expected. Tired and weepy. And she's likely to be going down to theatre in a matter of minutes now, so you might want to just say a quick hello for the moment, and come back tomorrow for a proper debrief. She'll be a different girl by tomorrow lunchtime, you'll see.'

'Has she said anything else to you?'

Sister Skaja shook her head. 'But that's because I haven't asked her. There's no rush. She isn't going anywhere, is she?' Then seeing my expression, which I knew conveyed the guilt I felt for asking, added, 'But if she does, I'll let you know, I promise.'

The curtains were drawn around the bed, because Adrianna had already been prepped for surgery – pre-op, bloods taken, attractive, bottom-revealing paper gown – and she didn't stir as I slipped between the gap. She was facing away from me, and I suspected she might be dozing – she must have been exhausted, after all. I wondered at her health again; how much of a brave face she might have been putting on for us. How I'd not properly registered how pale she always was.

I touched her lightly on the shoulder, and at first there was no response. But then she moved slightly and turned her head, and, in answer to my smile, her face crumpled and she immediately burst into tears.

I pulled the adjacent armchair across. It was surprisingly heavy. And noisy, as I dragged it across the hard hospital floor. It also took the curtain with it, revealing at least one patient who'd had a rude awakening. I made an apologetic face before pulling the curtain back.

'Oh, love,' I said, sinking down into the chair and taking Adrianna's nearest hand in my own. 'I wish you'd told me. I *so* wish you'd *told* me.'

She looked ghostly. Insubstantial. A wraith on the bed. And knowing what I now knew made me realise just how much worse-looking she *could* have been. No wonder she'd not been eating. No wonder she'd always been so pale, what with all the stress of her secret, and the anaemia and the infection. But the much greater pain that I knew she must have suffered. Was still suffering now. How could she not be? I remembered those first post-partum weeks as a time of both great joy and euphoria but also as a fog of anxiety and chronic, dragging pain.

All that. And among strangers. Perhaps terrified for her safety. Living with her heart in her mouth, and her nerves torn to shreds. And no baby. The trauma when Riley had suffered her miscarriage a couple of years previously was still vivid in my mind, and I knew it was in both Riley and David's too, so whatever had happened to this young girl I could definitely empathise.

No wonder she was wrung out. She certainly couldn't seem to stop herself crying right now. It was like a flood, all the tears she should already have shed having been finally been undammed. But for what? She'd had a baby. That we already knew. But what *had* become of it?

I plucked a tissue from the generic hospital box on the bedside cabinet and passed it to her, then let her hand go as she grabbed it and pressed it against her eyes. Her shoulders were still quivering.

'It's all right,' I said. 'Let it out. You're safe here. It's okay now. It's okay. Nothing bad's going to happen to you, sweetheart. You'll be down to theatre soon, and they'll make you better. Then you'll *feel* so much better. You wait and see. Everything will feel so much brighter in the morning.'

It didn't escape my notice that it was the sort of thing you'd say to a child who broke their dolly. But it was the best I could come up with in the face of her distress. And it was also true, for all that. She would.

'I'm so sorry,' she finally managed to articulate. 'I'm so sorry I lied to you, Casey. I was just so *scared*.'

'Shh …' I said. 'Shh … that's in the past now, okay? The important thing –'

'But I am. I am not a liar. I'm *so* sorry.' Then the tears again, the shoulders. It was heartbreaking to watch.

I leaned across and kissed her forehead. It was clammy. Soft and damp. 'Sweetheart, it's done now. You did what you thought you had to do. But it's *done* now. The important thing is for you to have your op and get better. No need to talk now. I'll be back tomorrow. We can talk then. No need to now. There's no rush …'

She gripped my hands. Both of them. Tightly. Almost violently. Just as I'd done the first day I'd met her. 'But my baby!' she whispered, tugging at me, urging me closer. 'Casey, my *baby*. I cannot bear it any more. I can't. I cannot go on. I have to find my little boy!'

Sister Skaja wasn't going to be on duty on Saturday morning but assured me that if I called at eight someone would be able to update me. In all likelihood it would be as she'd suggested would happen earlier; that Adrianna would have her op and her transfusion, and she'd feel a great deal better when she woke up. And I could return on Saturday lunch-time to see her. In fact, a porter was already on his way up to the ward to fetch her.

'And don't you worry,' she reassured me. 'She'll sleep like the proverbial dead tonight.'

Which I was pretty damned sure was going to be more than I'd do, I thought, as I hurried back down to the main concourse to hopefully stop Mike from coming out. There was no point. She needed nothing bar the skills of the medics. That, and sleep. I'd bring her stuff for her tomorrow. Much as I hated leaving her in such an emotional state, there was nothing I could do right now to help.

And in the meantime I could do little else but ruminate on the fact that everything we thought we knew about Adrianna wasn't so. And as I left the hospital two things immediately struck me. The first was that even if I couldn't sleep, I could at least now rest reasonably easy. Adrianna's baby was clearly out there somewhere and it was odds-on that we'd be able to find him.

And second – and this really brought me up short – that Adrianna's grasp of the English language was a great deal better than anyone had suspected.

Chapter 9

There are times when you despair of the human race. You watch some act of violence unfold on television, or read about a terrorist atrocity in a paper, or hear of some cruelty taking place scarily close to home, and suddenly it hits you. There are times when all the ill in the world seems to rear up and bite you, and when your faith in human nature can't help but plummet. I experienced one such nadir with Adrianna in the hospital the following afternoon.

Saturdays, in our house, were still sacrosanct. During the football season – and we were currently very much in the thick of it – no Saturday would be complete without some sizeable chunk of it being devoted to the beautiful game. Tyler went training in the mornings with the youth team he played for, and in the afternoon there would usually be some Kieron-related exodus, either to watch him play or coach his own team or referee.

And that was very much the way I still liked it. I've never been one for moaning about 'men and their football', because I've always enjoyed my Saturday afternoons too much, it having long since been clear that Mike didn't *do* shopping, and everyone was happier if I didn't make him.

And after getting over that hurdle, the weekends worked for everyone. I'd tootle around the shops with my sister – and, as the years passed, with our toddlers and then our children and then, eventually (and joyously) with our shopping-obsessed girl teenagers – while Mike inducted Kieron into the world of kicking balls round muddy fields.

Not so this afternoon. With Mike and Kieron off my hands, I'd invariably spend time with either Lauren or Riley, but this particular Saturday lunchtime saw me headed back to the hospital and, as I'd just managed to catch Mike the previous evening, carrying a weekend bag full of bits and bobs I thought Adrianna might need. And that included the paperback Tyler had bought her and which, if the page corner that was turned down didn't lie, she was already three-quarters of the way through.

I'd called the hospital first thing, as I'd been told to, and was put through to the ward, where I was told that the operation and transfusion had both been completed and that I should mosey up some time after one o'clock. Adrianna had slept well, apparently – which was probably no surprise to anyone – and as soon as I approached the bed I could see the change in her. She was clearly young enough to bounce back from the effect of the general anaesthetic, but more tellingly, she really did look as though a weight had been lifted. She was sitting up in bed, and there was a brightness to her skin that I had never seen before.

She frowned, nevertheless, as soon as I got to her.

'I am so sorry, Casey,' she began.

'Gawd,' I said. 'Don't start on that one again, please. You'll wear the flipping word out – in *both* languages!'

'I know, but I am,' she said. 'I cannot begin to tell you how much. You've been so kind to me, always. I hated to have to lie to you.'

I put the bag of clothes and toiletries down in front of the bedside cabinet. 'Sweetheart, I hate to know you felt that you *had* to,' I said, pulling the angry-sounding chair up to the bed again. '*Why* did you? Why were you so afraid to tell us the truth?'

Adrianna clasped her hands together in her lap, lacing her slender fingers together. Pianist's hands, my dad would have said. Pale and elegant. Ballerina's hands, I thought. Beautifully expressive. 'I did not know what to do,' she said. 'I was so frightened. I was so frightened I would be put in prison. That's why I said I was 14, because I have been told they do not put you in prison if you are 14.'

'But why would you think that anyway? Where did you get that from?'

'Because I have been in Britain illegally, for all this time now.'

'But you're from Poland ... which is in the EU – in Europe.'

'Because I came here illegally. I have no passport.' She pronounced it 'pass-e-port'. 'I know that now. There was a forged one. I never saw it. But it was forged. I know that now, too. And I do not know how now I can get one.

Whether I can even have one. Polish? English? But I am never going back. Never.'

Back. Not home. Back. No mention of home.

I said so. She nodded. 'No home. I have no home in Poland now, Casey. I have no one. Really. *No one.*'

'So,' I said, 'here I am. All ears.' I waggled them. She smiled a small smile. I smiled back, still a little bemused by the fact that this girl wasn't 14, but 16, and it suddenly made all the difference – though I couldn't for the life of me work out why.

I crossed my legs. 'So,' I said, 'how *did* you get to this point?'

And, in sometimes halting but always comprehensible English, Adrianna told me.

She'd told the truth when she told Marley Mae she came from the far north. She was from Gdansk, a Polish city on the Baltic Sea. Her father had been an industrial chemist and her mother a secretary, though, once Adrianna had come along, she had switched to working part time in a local wool shop. So far, so the fairy-tale, privileged child-hood. But then, when Adrianna was 11, her father had been killed in a big industrial accident and her and her mother's lives had changed overnight.

And changed radically. This was Poland at the start of the century. There was little in the way of a safety net, and with hardly any financial recompense her mother struggled to make ends meet. As a result, all the trappings of Adrianna's privileged childhood – including the piano lessons and the dancing, which she shyly admitted was a big part of her life, began falling away.

'So Lauren was right,' I said, remembering her commenting that Adrianna seemed good enough to dance professionally – in fact, almost as if she had already done so. 'You are a trained ballet dancer.'

'I won a scholarship,' she admitted, making mention of an academy whose name meant nothing to me. 'And for a time ...' She trailed off, seemingly lost in thought. 'But it is all in the past now. I could not continue. Because we moved.'

And move they did, her and her mother. To another part of Poland, down in the south, where her mother had the opportunity of working within a family business and, where, soon after, she met the man who was to become Adrianna's stepfather.

Adrianna's expression darkened as she described how quickly this man became the centre of her mother's world. And he had money too, which she said he used 'to control her'. To control both of them, it seemed, because, without him, they would have been a great deal worse off. 'On the street, he said. With nothing. But in whose eyes?' Adrianna asked me urgently. 'I had lost my father and now my mother. To him.'

She wavered then, her eyes filling up, but soon composed herself. I got the feeling anger was her form of self-defence. 'And then one day,' she continued, plucking idly at a loose thread on the hospital blanket, 'he told me I was old enough now, and that I had to earn my keep and help look after my mother. And so,' she continued, her voice clear and strong, 'he said that, from now, he was going to fuck me.' She raised her eyes to meet mine again. 'And so he did.'

I'm not easily shocked, for obvious reasons, but at that moment, in that setting, I think I actually gasped. Not so much by the fact of it – such calculated abuse is hardly unheard of, after all – but there was something so chilling in the calm way she reported this to me. As if it had become a memory, and a pain, that she'd long learned to accept.

And she seemed to have no concern about the choice of word, either. Were those his exact words to her? I suspected they might have been. I glanced around me, expecting to hear indignant huffs and puffs. I couldn't help it. But, thankfully, her voice was low enough to remain unheard; not least because of the average age on her part of the ward. Still, it brought it home to me that this apparently middle-class child (if such a thing existed in Poland) had come to the UK and learned her English from a very specific group of people – ones who'd throw such words into conversations without a thought.

And I suspected she'd followed the arc of my startled gaze, because she immediately reached out a hand to touch me.

'I'm sorry,' she said, also glancing at the women in the adjacent beds.

I realised then what had made my antennae so twitchy. Under the bright flush in her cheeks, she was broken. 'Oh, sweetheart ...'

It's okay,' she said quietly. 'It's okay, I am okay.'

* * *

There was, of course, the fact that we had only just scratched the surface, and with Adrianna still too queasy from the anaesthetic to think about eating lunch I was keen to hear the rest of her story.

Indeed, once the trolley had moved on, she seemed equally keen to get the lot of it – the whole lot of it – off her chest. She'd clearly been living with her terrible secrets for much, much too long.

She told me of how she initially felt complete disbelief. Of being in denial, of being raped and of finding it impossible to tell her mother. Of wondering if she should tell a teacher – she was by now attending the local middle school – but of fear of the repercussions paralysing her completely. He'd made repeated threats to her if she intended to say anything – didn't they all? I thought angrily – and she had no doubt that he would carry them out, either.

By now her maternal grandmother, with whom they'd first stayed, was growing elderly and in decline, victim to the ravages of dementia. And Adrianna quickly decided she couldn't hope for help there.

'So in the end,' she said, 'after six months or so, I found my courage and decided to tell my mother.'

I held my breath, knowing what was coming. Would have known anyway, even without Sister Skaja telling me. Because it so *often* happened. Which was why our city streets were paved not with gold but with homeless teenagers.

'She didn't believe me,' Adrianna confirmed. 'She thought I was making trouble. She told me I was jealous of her. She told me that I must never speak of it again.'

'And did you tell *him* – your stepfather – that you had told her?'

She nodded. Said in a small voice, 'I felt braver then.'

'And what happened?'

'He laughed. He had my mother – I think you have a saying – wrapped round his little finger. So I thought, I had two choices. To stay or to leave.'

'So you left. But where did you go? Didn't your mother try to stop you?'

Adrianna shook her head again. 'And it was okay that she didn't. It was better. To be away from him. For the first part, it was okay. For a small time I moved in with my grandmother. To help her. Which was good for her. And I still went to school.'

'You didn't think to tell a teacher?'

She looked at me as if I'd suggested something insane. 'No,' she said. 'No. He was a big man – big in the town there. Well known. I think people were scared of him.'

I nodded. It figured.

'No, I couldn't,' she went on. 'I dared not. And I didn't want to. I didn't know how it would help me. What it would achieve. And then my grandmother got sicker, and my uncles – who were far away – paid to move her to a home.'

'And you?'

'I ran away,' she said, once again clearly and calmly. 'I took money from my grandmother. I thought … I thought that she would not mind. Only a little money. Just enough. And then I went back to my house one day – I had a key to it still – and I found my birth certificate –'

'Which you still have?' That handbag. Which she guarded so carefully. Which, for all I knew, was kept safe under her pillow as she slept. Which I hadn't thought to look for when I'd gathered her things together. Why hadn't I? But it no longer mattered.

'I still have it,' she confirmed. 'Then I went on a bus to Krakow. I knew from the internet that there was a hostel there I could go to. So I went.'

I remembered what she'd originally told social services. 'You mean the children's home?'

'No.' She shook her head. 'No children's home. Just to a hostel.'

'And no one looked for you? Searched for you? Reported you missing?'

She shrugged. 'I don't know.'

'And your grandmother? Your uncles? You've had no contact with anyone?'

Her jaw jutted. 'My grandmother is gone for me. I know that.' I noticed her lower lip begin to tremble again. 'Casey, they can kick me out of here. It makes no difference. I am never going back. I have to stay. My baby …'

I grabbed the tissue box again.

I knew a lot about a lot – well, in my field of work, anyway. But I knew next to nothing about a whole lot else, obviously. And I knew very little about trafficking.

I racked my brains, vaguely recalling a course that Mike and I attended when we had very first decided to foster. That had been about trafficking – I was sure of it.

About men who preyed on vulnerable teens and promised them the world. Men who made them feel as if they were the only people in the world that truly understood and loved them, and then, when they got them hooked on the idea of the big romance, gradually started to break them down.

And 'break them down' – such a chilling term – was invariably the right one. These men were without scruples in destroying a girl's sense of self. They'd laugh at them, belittle them, make them feel inadequate – play with their hearts and their heads, worming away at their self-esteem, till they became completely dependent, unable to imagine life without them. Unable to imagine that they could even *survive* without them.

I remembered how, when I was young, I couldn't quite imagine how that happened. How one person could wield such immense power over another via such apparently resistible means. I couldn't, because I couldn't imagine it ever happening to me – if a man laughed at me, I'd laugh back. If a man insulted me, I'd ignore him. If a man tried to make me feel small, or so my thinking went, I'd simply consider him a loser and walk away from him.

But I'd lived and I'd learned, and I'd now worked with these kinds of teens, both as a foster carer and before that in a school. I'd have been fine because I wasn't vulnerable in that way – I'd had the privilege of a loving, supportive childhood. But they invariably didn't. Far from it. And that was key – these men knew exactly who to prey on, and the power that they wielded was very real. They could make these girls do anything, no matter how vile.

Because *they* were vile. They were scum. Barely human.

From what Adrianna told me, it sounded as though she'd been targeted and then painstakingly groomed. Which was no surprise to me, as she was such a striking girl. And also pliant – she was already vulnerable, being so far from home. Well, for the place that had once been home, anyway.

I seethed inwardly at the evil that had been done to her. Though, as always, at the same time I tried to be rational; tried to see the mother as the victim she undoubtedly was too. But it was hard, and I struggled to sympathise with a woman who refused to believe her own daughter; failed to understand how *she* could rationalise all that evil away.

It was a fool's errand even thinking about it. It was fact, and, as such, was unalterable. It was also testament to the power that a controlling sociopath – psychopath, even – could wield.

And so there Adrianna was – out of the frying pan and headlong into the fire. Which she soon found, in the form of an apparently nice guy, whom she met via a girl who had befriended her on her travels. A young man who had taken a shine to her, wanted a relationship with her and had promised her the world. Had promised, at the very least, that she could go with him to England, where she could work with him in the family shop and they could be together.

Of course, in reality, there was no 'family shop'. Just a knocking shop in a house somewhere out of the way in the

Midlands, apparently, where she was quickly disabused of her hopes for their romantic future, when she was billeted in a house with four other young girls, all of whom were being forced into prostitution.

I thought of Sister Skaja, who wasn't on duty today, but whose head I could see bobbing in my mind's eye, her hunch confirmed. 'So what did you do then,' I said, 'now you knew what was really happening?'

Adrianna shrugged. 'The same. I ran away again.'

'What about the police? Did you not think to go to the authorities?'

Again that look. Not disrespectful. I didn't think Adrianna was capable of it. Just the same surprise that I'd even think to ask such a thing.

'Never,' she said firmly. 'I thought they would put me in prison. That's what they do,' she added, leaning forwards, as if there might be police officers lurking behind the hospital curtains. 'They put people like me into detention centres. Another girl … one who was with us … That's what happened to her. She was never seen again.'

Or so she'd been *told*, I thought. By her captors – of course they would tell her that. So easy to terrify your teen-age slaves. 'So, what then? How did you manage to get away?'

'I went for milk one day …'

'You weren't physically held captive, then?'

She shook her head. 'I was told of some who were. We were told we would always be watched, and that if we tried anything they would always bring us back. But we weren't

Casey Watson

actual prisoners. A couple of the girls had to go to this other place. This brothel. Except we were prisoners, of course, because we all knew the alternative. We had no money, no immigration papers, no passport, no ID cards … but I had a little money, kept in secret, that no one knew about, and I used that. It is very cheap on the coaches to go a very long way. So I got on a bus.' She made a motion with her arms, as if she were running. 'It was at the bus stop, and I pretended to be walking past, then waited till the very last moment, before the doors shut. And I jumped on. Then another bus. To the city. Then on a coach. And went a long way away.'

'To London?'

She nodded. 'Eventually, yes, to London. I moved around a lot, at first. I was terrified they would find me. But then, in London, as the weeks passed, I began to feel safer. I had now made friends. And went to live with them. In a squatting house. You know squatting?' I said I did. 'And then it happened. I found out that I was pregnant.'

'By him. The man who brought you here?'

She nodded. 'Only him. Always. With the clients … It was still early and I told them I had an illness. That there were only some things I could do.' Her accompanying expression made it clear what sort of illness. So she'd been resourceful. Thank God. A small mercy.

'So, what then?'

She looked sad. 'My friends were so kind to me. They looked after me. They wanted me to go to the women's shelter they knew. But I couldn't. I dared not. I thought

114

they'd tell the police. Or that – I don't know – that he'd find me. That he'd know somehow, that I'd gone there. He'd told me of another girl. Who had run. And who he'd found in such a shelter …' She paused. 'So silly. I know that now. So silly. But I was so scared … That's why I told them I was 14. When I saw the people. So I'm too young to be taken to detention. I'm so sorry …' She plucked a handful of tissues from the box.

'And the baby?' I asked gently, while she blew her nose.

She crumpled the tissue, then began to twizzle it between and around her slender fingers. 'I had him in the big disabled toilet in that big park in London. The big one with the lake. The very famous one. There.'

So it could be one of two or three, I thought. Not that it mattered particularly. 'All on your own?'

She took another tissue. 'Not exactly. My girlfriend Ffion – she was the guard. To be sure no one came. She stole clothes for me. Because it was so, so cold. For the baby,' she added quickly. 'Only so he would be warm.' She said the words with such love.

I was about to ask – but *how*? How could a young girl – what must she have been by now? Fifteen? – how could a teenage girl simply lie down and give birth in such circumstances? I knew it happened – happened all over the bloody world, in fact, probably every minute – but I still couldn't quite get my head round what she'd done. What about the pain? What about the hygiene? What about the umbilical cord? The placenta? I knew I was a product of my own environment – a world of birth plans and hospitals and midwives and pain relief – but even that taken into account, I really, *really* couldn't begin to take it in.

I began to say so, but Adrianna was still deeply immersed in her memory. 'I cleaned him with baby wipes and dressed him in the new clothes. He was so beautiful, Casey. So perfect. So tiny. And I walked with him. It wasn't far.'

I was still stalled on the 'cleaned' bit. What about *her*? What about the placenta? What about the battleground between her legs? 'On your own?' I asked. 'Why on your own? Where was Ffion now?'

She shook her head. 'I made her go. I had to. Because I'd already decided what to do. She wanted me to go to hospital. She wanted for both of us to go to hospital. Me and the baby. There was one not so far away, she said. But I knew I couldn't go there. I dared not. I would be sent to detention and he would be taken from me anyway.'

I reached out and squeezed her hand. She was right. That would have been exactly what they'd have done. Not detention, no, but she and her child would most probably have been parted, because at 14 – assuming that's what she'd have told them – she would have been deemed too young to be able to look after him herself, and there were obviously no family members to call on for help. No question. They would have *had* to have separated them – what choice would they have had? Yes, the slim chance of a mother and baby placement, but where 'slim' equates to 'virtually no chance'. This mother and baby would therefore both have been assigned social workers – one for her, another for him, and he would have been spirited away to an emergency foster family forthwith. And she elsewhere. While enquiries ensued.

Which was the rub of it, really – though I wasn't about to tell her. Because if she'd told them her real age, i.e. old enough to work, there was a much higher chance that they *would* have been placed in foster care together – in a specialist family, as a mother and baby placement.

No, she mustn't know that. It would only upset her further. 'So?' I prompted, anxious to move on.

'So she agreed to go. I told her I would find somewhere for the baby and then return.'

'You didn't consider taking him back with you?'

'Not for a minute,' she told me seriously. 'It was not the right way. So I walked, and I found a box. By some recycling – it was a place with lots of offices. And I made a bed for him. It was still early morning. Not many people. Cold, but not so cold. And I took him into the police station.'

'And no one saw you go in?'

'I don't know,' she said. 'I don't think so. I did not wait to be caught. I left him just inside the swing door. And then I ran. Well –' She smiled a wan smile. 'As much as I *could* run, which wasn't much. And I got another coach. At Victoria. And I slept.'

'And ended up where?'

'Back in Hull. I knew Hull, so I went there.'

I was finding it difficult to keep up, because I kept coming back to the same thing. That she had just given birth. All this, having just been through labour. This slip of a girl, who had been through so much. Her presence of mind simply astounded me. 'Then what?' I said. 'What did you do once you got there? It's now, what? Evening?'

She thought for a second. 'Late afternoon,' she said. 'Dark. I found a place to buy coffee. Then I made my decision.'

'And found the council office?'

'Job Centre Plus,' she corrected. 'I went in and said I needed to find help, and they took me.'

I was intrigued, as much as anything by this turnaround in her plans. 'Your thinking being?'

She had obviously thought hard about it, too. 'That if I'd gone with the baby to the hospital they would take the baby away from me and send me back to Poland. That if I took my baby home I couldn't care for him, so he would get sick, and they would take him away from me and send me back to Poland. But if he was safe, and I could hide, I would at least be in the same country while I tried to decide what I must do to get him back again.'

Once again I found myself lost for words. So much on such slight shoulders. So incredibly much. But I realised there was a great deal of steel in there too. I'd been right. She had a plan to reinvent herself, clearly. To make a life, and a home, and, presumably, to work here. And then, at some point, to get her baby back again.

Then something occurred to me. 'But you didn't hide, in the end, did you? You didn't go back to your friends, like you told … Ffion, was it?' She nodded. 'Why not? Why not go back, once you'd made sure the baby was safe?'

Again she went quiet. Was it a decision she had agonised over? That she regretted?

'I am so sad for my friends. That I lied to them. Ffion very much. She was like a sister.' She sighed heavily. 'She is 15, you know. No home. It is so bad for her. But I knew it was not a good life for me with her – with *them*. I knew I … I just knew I was not *like* them. I couldn't stay.' She seemed to struggle to say this, and it suddenly made sense to me. That much as she was grateful to the people who had befriended her, theirs – a life of petty crime, homelessness, hopelessness, drug use – was not a life she wanted for herself. Having the baby would have made her think. Would have been a watershed for her. Still, she felt terribly guilty. I could see that so well.

'So,' I said, 'you went to the Job Centre, to seek help.'

'I just …' She seemed unable to find words. 'I just couldn't hide any more. It was so cold. So cold and frightening. It was – suddenly, there was no one. I couldn't do it any more. I had to go, but I was now alone. And I decided to take a risk. If I said I was 14, perhaps someone would agree to take care of me … I had heard of places, and people – *good* people – and I thought I must just *trust* … Great Britain, great people,' she added, trying hard to smile, but her face just refused to play ball. More tissues, more tears, a long, long moment of discomposure.

I stretched. My back was creaking. I hadn't realised how hunched up I'd been, listening so intently. 'Blimey,' I said, with feeling. 'All hail that Job Centre Plus, then!'

She nodded wanly through her tears, and dabbed furiously at her eyes again. 'Because they brought me to you. You and Mike. And lovely Tyler. Which I do not deserve. And I've … I'm so … so …' She held the tissue to her mouth and choked back another sob.

We both heard the rattle of the trolley before we saw it. 'What can I get you, love? Tea? Coffee? Milk? Glass of squash?'

None of the above, I thought. *Just her baby*.

Just her *baby*. Just that one little thing, really. No biggie.

Chapter 10

Over the rest of the weekend the dust began to settle on this astonishing new reality, but, at the same time, it was a lot to take in. It seemed Adrianna was going to be kept in hospital until the Tuesday and, in the meantime, Mike and I agonised over how much, if anything, we should tell Tyler.

We knew the drill – we'd dealt with similarly emotionally complex situations with Riley and Kieron (especially Kieron), and had been trained in some of the issues around such situations too. And Mike had already paved the way for things anyway; after speaking to me on the phone on the Friday evening he had prudently stuck to the basics with Tyler. All he'd told him was that it appeared that Adrianna's time sleeping rough had finally caught up with her. That she'd collapsed, having been badly and chronically anaemic, but that once she'd had her transfusion she would be fine.

Tyler would obviously now have to be told something more than this, though, and he'd need to know sooner rather than later. After all, he was no longer a child who could be whisked off to bed before the grown-up conversations took place. He was old enough to know, and *should* know, at least the bulk of what had happened, and, with the comings and goings that would result from these new developments, he would need to know the full picture going forward, as well.

There was also the small matter of how he felt about Adrianna, which had become increasingly obvious to both of us. He had something of a crush on her – there was no doubt about it. And this news would throw all that out of kilter. We had no idea *how* it would affect things between them. Only that it would. And it was important that we be prepared for that.

'But you know what?' I said to Mike when we were alone on the Saturday evening (Tyler being at the cinema, seeing some superhero movie with his friends). 'It's felt a bit like that in any case – you know? A bit like an infatuation from the get go, don't you think? Even when we thought they were around the same age.'

'They're not so very different in age *anyway*,' Mike pointed out. 'He'll be 15 in a matter of months now, and we still don't know when Adrianna was 16.'

'I never thought to ask her that,' I mused. 'Of all the things I asked her, I never thought to ask her that one. Isn't that strange?'

'Not really,' Mike said. 'I'd say you had a lot more pressing questions to ask her.'

'Hey, there's a thought,' I said, grabbing my mobile to check the time. 'When's that take-away supposed to be coming? (That was a bit of an oddity too. That we still called it a 'take-away' when more often than not these days it was actually a 'deliver-to'.)

'Twenty minutes or so. Why?' Mike looked at me suspiciously. 'What's on that mind of yours?'

'A bit of sleuthing.'

'*Really*?'

'*Yes*, really. So don't look at me like that, because I don't see the harm. Look, she told me she'd got her birth certificate hidden somewhere, didn't she? And where is it going to be? In her handbag. So I'm going to find it. Why not?'

Mike rolled his eyes. 'You are seriously telling me you are going to go rummaging in her bedroom like a common thief?'

'Yes, I am seriously telling you,' I confirmed. I stood up, decided. 'Look, what's going to be the first thing she does when she's home again? Get out her birth certificate for us. So where's the harm? At least we'll have *one* thing about her that we know is true. Anyway, I've got to update John, haven't I? And presumably get something in motion about finding the baby for her. So as far as I'm concerned, the sooner we have some facts to work with the better. There'll be information on there that he probably needs, won't there? Information about where she was born, and who her parents are and who knows what else?'

Mike raised his hands. 'All right, all right – you can stop trying to convince me, Sherlock. Go do your sleuthing, with my blessing.'

* * *

I was telling Mike the truth, too. As the day had gone on, and I'd began to absorb the enormity of what Adrianna had told me, I'd felt increasingly bullish about taking charge of a situation that, up to now, I'd had as much control over as I would have had over a runaway horse. Nevertheless, it felt strange going into Adrianna's bedroom to snoop about. So strange that it struck me just how fully she'd inhabited it, and how completely we'd fallen in with her wishes in that regard. It was partly due to her age, of course, and my sensitivity to her right to privacy, but perhaps we'd been giving her too much for her own good.

With other, younger children, I wouldn't have thought twice about it in a similar situation, particularly if I had cause to be concerned that they might be hiding something with which they could do themselves, or another person, harm. Children who'd spent time in care, or in dangerous, insecure home situations, often learned to be secretive and sometimes sly. I could recall many situations where my occasional 'sleuthing' sorties bore both physical and/or emotional fruit. Which was not to say that I didn't respect our foster children's privacy; simply that, on occasion, it was necessary to follow my instincts and go further than what was obvious on the surface.

But this hadn't been the case with Adrianna. It really had seemed almost as if she'd been a paying lodger, rather than a foster child we were in loco parentis for.

And now we knew the truth about her age, another thought struck me – we'd never fostered a 'child' of 16 before. And Adrianna had been right in her assessment of what would have happened to her if she'd come clean about her age from the beginning. At 16, it was unlikely she'd have been sent to a family, because the pressure on the service was simply too great. She'd more likely have been dealt with as would any vulnerable minor, and been put in some emergency bed and breakfast place.

It always tickled me, that. The way the name 'bed and breakfast' still persisted. Because in reality, though beds and breakfasts were obviously a part of it, such places bore almost no resemblance to most people's understanding of what a B and B would be. There would be no jolly landlady wielding a fish slice, for starters. No hearty breakfasts, no seaside, no residents' lounge, no benign, kiss-me-quick, holiday-postcard feel.

No, 'B and B', in this context, was a completely different animal. A room, with a Yale lock, in a house full of similar rooms, variously occupied by such members of society's flotsam and jetsam as were lucky enough not to sleep on the streets or on a cheap bunk in a down-at-heel hostel. Not that any luxury could be expected. It would be a run-down house, too – probably in a hard-to-rent area, where only the hard lingered – with a largely absent landlord, and some meagre food offering in order to qualify for the necessary box-ticking with the council. It would be grim. It would be bleak. It would be horrible.

And gentle Adrianna could so easily *be* there. The notion struck me forcibly as I pushed open the bedroom door. Had she come clean about her age when she'd trusted her fate to our social services, it was where she so easily could have been.

I inhaled the smell of her. Which I realised was the smell of my current fabric conditioner. Brightly floral. Vaguely antiseptic. Pleasant. She could be *there*, if she had told them. Not in our sunny back bedroom. She could be in some dismal B and B place, with all hope bleeding away, and her thin veneer of optimism peeling away like the wall-paper. And how long, it then struck me, before distress turned to desperation? Desperation to depression? Independence to vulnerability to God-knew-what kind of predators? And the whole distressing cycle began again?

No, there was no question that, in lying about her age, Adrianna had done the right thing. She had saved her baby. And then, showing a presence of mind that still astounded me, she'd done something remarkable, unlikely and nigh-on impossible. She had also saved herself.

It felt slightly shameful that I located Adrianna's handbag so easily. For all that she must have trusted no one when she'd arrived with us, the passing of the weeks had probably helped lower her defences; she probably never imagined I'd go looking for it. And there it was, almost as predicted – not quite under her pillow, but not far away. It was tucked beneath the mattress. She'd not taken it with her to Lauren's dance class because she really had no need to. With Lauren picking her up, then the class, then Lauren dropping her off home again – well, in theory – there would have been no point in taking it.

I pulled it out, and considered the lack of weight in my hands. It felt as if there wasn't anything in it. She'd wrapped the shoulder strap around it and, as I unravelled it, I wondered just how far it might have travelled.

Inside, there was very little. An almost empty travel pack of tissues, a couple of twizzled hair elastics, a small plastic tail comb and a coin purse that was embroidered with the London skyline. This I opened too, to find no more than a couple of pounds' worth of loose change; no wonder, if this paltry sum reflected her monetary all, that she had arrived in Hull and thrown herself at its mercy.

No wonder, anyway. She'd been immediately post-partum, hadn't she? So she must have been in some pain, presumably exhausted, starving hungry and very cold. And the one thing she *did* have – the friends she had made in London – she had decided, for her baby's and her own sake, to relinquish. I still wasn't sure I followed her slightly cock-eyed logic, but I didn't doubt her sincerity for a moment. Neither did I doubt that she'd done the right thing. How quickly would she have gone under if she'd returned to that squat? She'd have been babyless, heartbroken, physically at a low ebb. She'd not mentioned any dalliance with drugs or alcohol, and she didn't look as if she'd had a drug habit, but how soon before the consolations of chemical oblivion would begin to look beguiling?

The only other item in the bag, as far as I could see, was a chapstick. No birth certificate or any other form of paperwork. I looked carefully, sleuthfully, even felt around the lining, but there was no sign that it had even been tampered with.

So if the birth certificate wasn't in there, she must have stashed it somewhere else. And logic told me it would be secreted among the possessions she'd brought with her. She was too bright a girl to have hidden it in the fabric of the house. And probably right not to do so, if that had indeed been her logic – according to her thinking, once she'd confessed and made her true position known to us, there was as much chance of her never being allowed back here as there was of her being able to come home again.

I went to the wardrobe and opened it, seeing the few items of clothing it contained, and felt a pang of compassion, thinking of her lying there in hospital, having finally confessed everything, and, despite my assurances (after all, she'd been lied to before), wondering what was going to become of her now. And missing her baby. The ever-present agony of her loss must be so visceral, and I was reminded of a book I had recently read about a young unmarried mother who'd been forced to hand over her baby for adoption, and how eloquently she described the intensity of her pain.

The leather jacket, then. It called to me. She would have hidden it in her leather jacket. Her traffickers could, and probably did, search her handbag. All their power lay in making her powerless, by being paperless. But they'd perhaps not think of searching the lining of her coat.

And, within a matter of moments, I had my hands on it. A much-folded piece of paper, closely wrapped in thin plastic – perhaps a slip case for a student ID card or some such, and inserted, via a neat slit, under the chunky, biker-style lapel. I carefully eased it out, feeling even more like a criminal, and grateful for the breadth of my pre-fostering career. Working in a comprehensive school and, prior to that, with vulnerable teens and young adults, I too had done my flotsam and jetsam years.

'Car pulling up!' Mike's voice, from the foot of the stairs.

'Coming now!' I called back, putting the jacket back in the wardrobe, and closing the bedroom door before rattling back down the stairs with my booty.

'Got it,' I said, brandishing it, once he'd paid the delivery driver.

'And?' Mike said, following me into the kitchen with the goodies.

I slipped the document from its plastic sheath and carefully unfolded it. 'Adrianna Aleksandra Rudzinski, born in Gdansk – ah, so that detail *was* true – on, let me see … oh my word, look at that!'

'Look at what?'

I thrust the paper in front of him. '*That.*'

'That being what?'

My husband, for all his fine attributes, wasn't perfect. 'That,' I said. '*Look*. At the *date*, stoopid! Adrianna has the same birthday as Marley Mae!'

Mike looked, finally registering. Dates weren't his forte. 'So you've decided there's some spooky significance to that, have you?'

'Derrrr,' I teased. 'Don't be daft. Though, actually, come to think of it … *No*, silly,' I said, grinning. 'I'm thinking *party!*'

I had thought it would be most appropriate to leave the call to John till Monday – whatever he'd said, his weekend was still his weekend, after all. But Sunday morning brought news of Adrianna's marked improvement and the fact that I could pick her up on Monday instead, and I decided that, with so much new information to impart, I'd better put John in the picture before I went to fetch her.

With Mike and Tyler safely ensconced in the living room in front of the telly, I called him that afternoon and told him all. I'd already logged everything I could remember, because I wanted to get it down while it was still fresh in my mind, but I was keen to run it all past John as well.

'So it looks like we need to allocate that social worker now, doesn't it?' he said, once I'd finished giving him chapter and verse on Adrianna's life story.

'And the local constabulary, and Interpol, and possibly Sherlock Holmes, while you're at it. John, we *have* to track down her baby for her.'

He chuckled. 'Just like that, eh?'

'Just like that. How hard can it be, after all? As soon as she has identified the police station where she left him, it's surely only a matter of following the paper trail, isn't it? Which surely can't be that long. They'll have called the local social services office, who'd have gone and collected him, and if they didn't take him to the nearest hospital –

actually, that's exactly what they'd have done, isn't it? Might even have put an appeal out on the local TV. In fact, I'll bet they'll have done that too, don't you? Anyway, *after* that, they'd have placed him with a local foster family while they waited for someone to come forward to claim him – simples!'

'No, you're right,' John said, 'it shouldn't be too difficult at all.' He paused. A pregnant pause. Which I might well have pointed out to him, while chortling, had his next utterance not sounded as ominous as it did. '*That* bit of it will be simple, at any rate,' he said. 'Casey, don't leap too far ahead here. Especially where the girl's concerned. The next bit might not be quite so straightforward.'

'But she's 16, John,' I pointed out, belatedly aware of where this was leading. 'Not 14. *Sixteen*. So –'

'So, yes, in theory that makes a huge difference. And obviously, reuniting mother and baby is the outcome everyone would hope for. But it's by no means cut and dried. Specially given the paucity of information we have about her and where she came from.'

'But we *do* now.'

'Not exactly. She's come into the country without a passport, illegally. There's a lot still to know. A *lot*. Before they'd even consider doing any considering.'

'John, I know that. I'm not daft. I know it's all going to take time.'

'I know you do. I'm just reminding you. So you can spell it out to her. You know what they are going to say. That they have a duty of –'

'Care. Yes, I know all that too.'

'And this is a whole other council we're talking about, don't forget. And the baby is settled where he is and presumably thriving. I just don't want her getting her hopes up that getting her child back is a foregone conclusion. There might be some major hoops to jump through …'

'John, stop stressing. I know all of that too. Though you don't know her like I do. Trust me, she will be capable of looking after him.'

'You can't be that sure,' he pointed out. 'You've only had her with you a few weeks. And, more pertinently, you've just begun being able to have proper conversations with her!'

'John, it's not about talking. It's instinct. She's a decent kid. I know she is.'

'One who's allegedly been *abused*, Casey. And *trafficked*. There might be a great deal you *don't* know.'

I sighed. I knew full well why John had to run all this past me. 'Hey,' I said, 'is this the five-minute lecture or the full half-hour?'

He laughed. '*Me?* Lecture *you?* I wouldn't be so presumptuous! Seriously, though –'

'Seriously, John. You don't need to worry. I *do* know. And I know you have to make sure I don't forget it. And I promise I shall be sure to *make* sure that I manage her expectations.'

I then added another 'simples!' to reassure him that I would. And made a mental note to myself that I must stop using that expression. I was getting way beyond the point of wearing it out.

And, as it turned out, it was anything but simple.

Chapter 11

'What a difference a couple of days make!' Sister Skaja said when I arrived on the ward the following day. 'She hardly seemed like the same girl when I came in this morning. Bright eyed, bushy tailed – what a transformation! Suspect the blood might have helped too,' she added, grinning at me. 'And, of course, she's been chattering nine to the dozen to everyone, apparently ...'

Sister Skaja was sitting at the nurses' station, pen in hand. She took her bright turquoise reading glasses off and shoved them carelessly into her hair. She then reached across the counter and touched my arm, grinning again. 'You and your family get several mentions in dispatches, I can tell you. *Seriously*,' she added. 'Bless her. You should think about starting a fan club. You'll definitely be needing to polish your halo.'

I could feel the colour rising in my cheeks, which didn't happen very often. Neither did those awkward moments when you have absolutely no idea what to say in reply. I settled on, 'Well, we have *so* much to thank *you* for. If you'd not been on duty Friday night ... And been so kind, and so helpful ...'

She raised both hands in front of me, her smile turning to a chuckle. 'Okay, touché! We'll stop all this now, shall we? She's hot to trot. So, go on. Go and fetch her home. *And* that baby of hers,' I heard her add as I walked away.

I'm not really one for the paranormal or magic or any of that stuff, but when I pushed back the curtain around Adrianna's bed (after calling out 'It's only me!' just in case she was only half dressed) I just had this sixth sense that all wasn't well. Hard to explain – just this slight 'oh no' feeling, when I saw her empty bed.

I pushed the curtain back more fully, and looked up and down the ward. Plenty of hospital staff milling about, but no sign of her.

I walked back to the nurses' station, thinking she'd perhaps gone to wait in the day room, but as I passed the nearest occupied bed I stopped to ask the lady in it if she'd seen her. Might as well.

'Adrianna?' I said, gesturing back towards the other bed. 'The girl in the bed next to you? The Polish girl? Do you know where she is?'

The woman, who was very elderly, craned her neck a little. Then she mumbled something.

'Sorry?' I said. She raised a finger in the air and flapped it vaguely.

'She went to get dressed,' called the woman opposite. 'Don't worry about her. She probably can't hear you,' she added, nodding her head towards the elderly woman.

'Oh, I see,' I said, feeling stupid for having had such a dozy premonition. Of *course* Adrianna would have gone off to get dressed.

'Thank you,' I said to the elderly lady anyway, and went across to where the other woman was sitting up in her own bed. She was wearing a floral winceyette nightie, and was knitting.

'It's a scarf,' she said, even though I hadn't asked her. 'I told your girl … well, I know she's not *actually* your girl, obviously …'

'I'm her foster carer,' I quickly supplied. The feeling wasn't going away.

'That's it,' the woman said. 'She did explain, bless her. I told her I'd make her one of these if she was staying in here long enough. I rattle through them like nobody's business, I do. I get this bobbly wool from down the market,' she added, fingering the heap of tufty knitting in her lap. 'Two pounds a ball, that's all it is. Knits up lovely, doesn't it? I told her I'd make her a nice one in reds and browns – go with that lovely hair of hers.'

She shifted the pile in her lap again, which was blue. 'Well, that's if my daughter was coming anytime soon,' she said, 'which she isn't – she's a legal secretary, you see, out in the business park. She nips down and gets it me. Still, never mind. It's not like you can't buy them for peanuts these days in Primark, is it? But it passes the time.

The days drag when you're in hospital, don't they?' She nodded towards Adrianna's bed. 'Lovely girl, she is. Such a shame.'

The woman didn't elaborate on what aspect of it being 'a shame' she was aware of. 'She is indeed,' I said, casting my gaze around the ward again, the strange feeling of anxiety still refusing to leave me. 'Where would she have gone? D'you know? You know, to get dressed and that?'

'Disabled toilet,' the woman said, knitting furiously as she spoke. 'Makes sense, doesn't it? Plenty of room in there. Down by the ward entrance, it is.'

I nodded. 'Of course. I think I'll wander down then … anyway, thank you,' I added. 'Happy knitting.'

First, however, I went back to Adrianna's bed. I looked around. There seemed to be nothing of hers left there. Just the big plastic water jug, which was half full and had formed thousands of bubbles against the sides.

I opened the door in the bedside cabinet. There was nothing in there either. So she'd obviously taken the backpack Mike had filled with her toiletries and night things. It was an old one of Tyler's. Black, with a Nike swoosh.

I sat quietly on the noisy chair, and waited for a good five or ten minutes. Perhaps she was putting on some make-up. Maybe doing her hair.

But when a further ten minutes had passed, I went back to the nurses' station, where Sister Skaja was still sitting, drinking tea and sorting through some paperwork.

'All set?' she asked. Then looked behind me. 'Oh. Where's Adrianna?'

I waved a hand back towards the ward. 'The lady opposite says she's gone to get ready,' I explained. 'But she's certainly taking her time about it. If that's what she *is* doing. Have you seen her?'

Sister Skaja put her pen down. 'No. No, I haven't. Not since she went to get changed.' She rose and looked down towards the ward entrance, the view of which was partly obscured by an elderly couple shuffling along, and a nurse pushing a drugs trolley.

'The lady told me she might have gone to change in the disabled toilet,' I said. I was starting to feel slightly panicked now. Properly panicked even. Sister Skaja came round from behind the counter.

'She might well have,' she agreed. 'For the mirror. In fact, I think she said she was going to do exactly that. Have you checked?'

I shook my head. Sister Skaja passed me and headed off, striding purposefully, to a wide toilet door about three down, by the swing doors.

It was shut, but she pushed it. 'Vacant,' she said. 'And also empty. So where …' She pushed open another door, this time marked 'Patient Toilet'. And underneath that, 'Visitors are respectfully reminded that these facilities are for the use of patients ONLY. Public facilities are available in the main hospital reception and in Muffins cafeteria.'

'Also empty,' Sister Skaja observed. 'Might she not have gone back to her bed?'

I told her Adrianna hadn't. Well, at least, that I didn't think she could have passed me without my seeing her.

'Her bed's at the end,' I added, the ominous feeling still refusing to go away.

'Well, in that case,' Sister Skaja said, 'I'm stumped. Ah – unless she's gone to wait for you in the day room, that is.'

We duly trooped across to the day room. 'But then I'd have seen her myself, surely?' she mused. 'And I'm pretty sure I didn't. So,' she said, as we went back to the nurses' station once again, 'she's either gone off somewhere else to wait for you, or … well, I really have no idea. So perhaps that's it. Perhaps she's gone to wait for you down in the main reception. That'll be it, I imagine. Don't you?'

I told Sister Skaja I thought she was probably right, all the while feeling certain she was probably wrong. That hadn't been the plan. I was to come up and fetch Adrianna from the ward, and she'd have known that. She'd have been given her chit from the pharmacy, or …' Another thought hit me.

'Ah. Did she have to go and get her drugs, perhaps?' I asked, feeling just a small spark of hope. 'Her antibiotics?'

Sister Skaja shook her head. 'No, they were brought up to her earlier, just after the doctor's round.'

'Well, she's obviously gone downstairs to wait for me, like you said,' I agreed. I felt a powerful urge to go looking for her now. 'No worries!' I said, smiling brightly. 'I'm sure I shall track her down!'

I didn't. I looked everywhere I could imagine Adrianna could conceivably be waiting for me. I checked Muffins, the main reception and the A&E reception. I checked the little place with the vending machines round the corner from A&E. I checked the coffee bar that was on the far side of the main reception, plus the newsagents, the WRVS shop and the paved area outside that sternly said 'No Smoking' but where, late at night, I knew patients sneaked down and smoked nevertheless. Then I walked out to the car park, hoping that by some miracle she'd be out there, wandering around, looking for my car.

She wasn't. So when I reached it I clicked the remote and opened it, slung my bag on the driver's seat and ferretted about in it for my mobile.

Mike's phone rang several times before he answered, and I used the time to keep scanning the car park.

'What's up, love?' he said, sounding concerned. I generally tried not to phone him at work.

'It's Adrianna,' I told him. 'She's disappeared.'

'*What*? How could she disappear?'

'That was precisely my question.'

'What – from the ward? I thought you'd arranged a time to pick her up?'

'I had. And they said she'd gone off to get dressed, ready. And then – pfft! – she disappeared.'

'You sure you've checked everywhere? Sure you didn't miss each other on one of those corridors?'

'No. At least, I don't think so. Why would she even leave before I got there? The plan was that I'd come up to the ward and fetch her, wasn't it?'

'So maybe she got confused …'

'I don't know, Mike. I just have this *feeling* …'

'What feeling?'

'I don't know. I just don't think she would have done that. She'd have waited for me. Why would she wander off on her own?'

'Assuming she has. Couldn't she just be in the toilet or something?'

I explained about the knitting woman, who'd been pretty clear that Adrianna had gone off to the disabled toilet to get dressed. 'And never came back again,' I finished.

'Because she then went straight down to meet you,' he said. 'That makes sense. That'll be it. Perhaps she got it wrong. Why don't you go back to reception and ask them?'

'I suppose,' I said. 'I'll do that. Oh, but Mike, why do I have such a bad feeling about this?'

'I have no idea,' he said. 'Why *do* you?'

'I don't know. I just *do*. She's not stupid. Why on earth would she go rattling round the hospital?'

'I have no idea,' he said again. 'To grab a coffee? To make a phone call?'

'She doesn't have any money.' And as I said that, the thought soothed me. But the feeling was only momentary. I didn't actually know that at all, did I? 'I'll go back in,' I told Mike. 'Have another rootle around.'

'Okay,' he said. 'Keep me posted. Don't worry, love. You'll find her.'

'I hope so,' I said when I rang off.

I didn't.

* * *

The sky was threatening rain when I walked back across the car park to the hospital entrance. If I'd had a bad feeling when I'd found Adrianna's bed empty, I had a *very* bad feeling now. And nothing I saw or heard made it better. I went straight back up to the ward to find that Sister Skaja was apparently on her break, but it soon became clear, because the nurse I asked went and asked everyone she *could* ask, that Adrianna hadn't returned to the ward. 'She's been discharged,' the nurse said reasonably. 'So why would she?'

I then retraced my steps – back to the café, back to the other café, back to the vending machines and shops – and finally joined the enquiries queue back in the main reception. And, after ten minutes that felt like at least twenty, I asked the woman there if she remembered seeing Adrianna at all.

It was a ridiculous question – what must the footfall be in this hospital concourse? Twenty people per second passing through? At the very least, I imagined. Still, I had to try. 'Tall and pretty,' I said. 'Polish. Long dark brown hair. Very *long* dark brown hair,' I qualified. 'Down past her waist.' Well, hopefully, I thought, remembering the hair scrunchie still in her handbag.

'I've not seen her, love,' she said. 'Not that I can remember anyway. In the last half hour, you say?'

'Around that,' I said. 'Maybe longer.'

'Well, if she was after getting the hospital transport, or a bus, she'd have probably gone out that way.' She pointed. 'See that man over there? In the purple fleece? Balding?' I nodded. 'You might want to ask him. He's one of our retired meeters and greeters. He might have seen her. You never know.'

I duly hurried across, and, again, had to wait in a small queue, while he directed various people to various places.

'And what can I do for you?' he said brightly, once my turn came.

Once again I explained who I was looking for, and described her.

'Polish, you say?' he said, scratching his head with the corner of his clipboard. 'Foreign, then, is she?'

I nodded. 'Yes. Do you think you saw her?'

'Might have,' he said, looking pleased with himself suddenly. 'Well, if it's the one I'm thinking of. Bonny lass. Tall. Was after a bus.'

'After a bus?'

'Well, like I said, if it *was* her. I'm not saying it definitely was, mind. But she *was* tall and she was bonny …'

'Carrying a backpack, by any chance?'

'I couldn't say, love. No, wait. I think she *was* carrying a bag, come to think of it. I remember her hands being round the straps – you, know – thinking it's cold out, and that.' He slipped the clipboard under his arm and rubbed his own hands together. It *was* cold. Especially with the automatic doors pinging open and shut all the time. It couldn't have been a very restful place to work. But perhaps being retired, that was what he liked about it.

'So a bus to where exactly?' I asked him, mentally crossing my fingers. 'Did she say?'

'Just to town, love,' he said, pointing to a bus that was just arriving. 'One of them. Hope you catch up with her!' he trilled as I hurried off.

I called Mike again, once I'd climbed back into the car. 'She's got on a frigging bus!' I wailed at him. 'Can you *believe* it? What's she *doing*?'

'Well, if it *was* her –'

'I'm sure it must have been. The man I spoke to seemed pretty certain.'

'Well, not home then, evidently. Not if she's got on a bus to town.'

'So *where* then?' I stopped. I had just answered my own question. 'She's bolted again, hasn't she?'

'Bolted?'

'Run *away*. Run away from *us*, Mike!' I still couldn't quite believe it.

'But why?'

'Because … Because – God, I don't *know*. Why would she *do* that? Why now? When she's confessed everything to me. When she's told us the truth? It just doesn't make any sense.'

'Perhaps it does,' Mike said. 'Perhaps that's precisely *why* she's done a runner. Because she wasn't exactly planning on the truth coming out, was she? She had no choice but to confess, did she? And now she's thought about everything, perhaps she's scared –'

'Scared of what? Of us? Christ, we've done nothing but offer her a home and some breathing space. What exactly does she have to be afraid of?'

'Of everything. What's going to happen to her. What's going to happen to her when she leaves us. She must have been thinking about it – you know, what the repercussions might be. Who knows what she's been thinking, love? We've barely been able to make sense of her up till now. Course, that's if she *has* done a runner. Which you don't actually know yet … How d'you know she hasn't just got herself confused? How d'you know she hasn't, I don't know, taken it upon herself to pay a visit to the shopping mall on her way home?'

'Mike, stop being ridiculous! She *knew* I was coming to get her. And besides, she has never been anywhere without me, has she? Or Lauren or Tyler being with her – Mike, she wouldn't know where to start!'

'You don't know that for definite. Perhaps the message got confused.'

'How could it? What's so difficult about whatever nurse it was I spoke to telling her I'd be picking her up this lunchtime? Besides,' I added, shutting the car door and putting the key in the ignition, 'she doesn't have any money.'

'Ah,' he said. 'But she must do. If she's got on a bus.'

'But where would she have got it *from*?'

'Who knows? What's that noise?'

'The car.' I'd started the engine. And it had come to me finally. What her plan might have been. 'I'm going to go and try to find her,' I told Mike.

He exhaled. 'How exactly can you do that when you don't know where she's gone?'

'I think I do. If she's running away, where's the most likely place she'd head to?'

'I don't know. You tell me.'

'The *coach* station,' I said, swivelling round to grab the seatbelt. My hunch was fast resolving into a definite conviction. 'I know what's she's thinking.'

'Case,' Mike said, 'isn't that just the *point*? That we've *never* known what she's been thinking?'

I knew that. As I pulled out of the car park it really started falling into place for me – that Adrianna had been a mystery from day one. That we'd spent all these weeks managing to learn absolutely nothing about her – nothing. She'd fooled everyone. And now? I didn't have a clue.

But I did have a *clue*. 'I get the coach.' Wasn't that what she'd said? Something like that, anyway. That was it, I remembered. *It is very cheap on the coaches to go a very long way.*

It was a long shot. But the only shot I had of catching up with her. And as I turned onto the dual carriageway it didn't feel like a terribly long shot at all, not when I scrolled back though all the other things she'd said to me. *I don't deserve … I feel so guilty … my friend Ffion … like a sister almost …* She would be bound for London. Definitely. I'd have staked my life on it.

Chapter 12

Not having a sat nav, I had to drive mostly on memory and instinct, just like they did in the olden days. And when that failed – when I was halfway round my third confusing roundabout – I realised that there was nothing for it. I would have to use my mobile.

I pulled in at the next layby (which was a bus stop, but I had no time for by-laws) and, after spending some time trying to remember all the lessons Kieron had taught me about how to use the 'maps function', remembered that I could just go online instead, via my browser, type in 'coach station' and hopefully pin the place down. That was what the GPS thing was there for, wasn't it?

I did at least know the coach station – I'd seen both kids off on various school and college adventures from it over the years – but, as is often the case, when you're in a flap, and coming from the other side of a sprawling city, I had little idea how to get there from where I was.

My route was also complicated by the web of city-centre one-way systems that had, in recent years, started to spring up all over the place. And could, I knew, send me hurtling off anywhere. But luck was with me, it seemed, because no sooner had I typed it than the local coach station – well, a map showing where it was, apparently – popped up on screen, and even asked me if I'd like some directions. And, having perused them, I was at least half-sure of where I was going, and a comforting three-quarters sure of where I currently was.

Even so, it was a fraught drive, because my mind was now racing despite the reassuring tones of the treacle-voiced navigator who lived in my phone. Suppose I was wrong? Suppose Adrianna hadn't decided to go back to London? Suppose she was planning on going somewhere different altogether? Suppose – and now I did have to rein myself in, sternly – the man or men who'd trafficked her *had* tracked her down? Suppose she'd gone with them, under duress?

I chided myself – that couldn't happen, surely? Someone would have seen something, no question. You couldn't just walk onto NHS wards and abduct 14-year-old girls. No, 16-year-old girls, I corrected myself, remembering.

But then a new thought occurred to me. Mike was right. We barely knew Adrianna. We had formed impressions, that was all, based on shared culture and values. Who was to say any of those impressions were correct?

There was also the matter of Adrianna's access to the internet. No, she might not have a phone, but she'd know as much about the web as the next savvy teenager. Who was to say that she hadn't befriended all sorts on social media? Who was to say she wasn't still in touch with her old friends?

That thought reassured me. I was certain that if she was headed anywhere it would be London – the way she'd spoken of her friend Ffion, and how bad she'd felt leaving her and lying to her. Now, perhaps, she felt some compulsion to return to her. To take her chances. To evade the spectre of all that 'detention centre' nonsense.

I was now at least in a road system I recognised more confidently. And though the traffic was heavier, I began to feel hopeful. I couldn't be more than five minutes from the coach station and I reckoned she couldn't have more than, say, a 40-minute start on me. And what were the chances of her fetching up there and of a coach bound for London leaving immediately? They surely didn't run more than one coach an hour, did they?

If she was even going there, of course.

Life is full of irritations, isn't it? Things not going the way you want them to. Petty inconveniences are part of life, and it doesn't do to get your knickers in a twist over them. Parking, in my case, wasn't terribly often one of them. Yes, I had the odd huff in the odd supermarket car-park situation, and I was as impatient as the next person in the weeks running up to Christmas, when you couldn't get a space in the multi-storey for love or money. But, on a day-to-day basis, parking issues didn't tend to be *my* issues, so when I turned into the coach station and was immediately waved at, I thought that waving – just waving – was exactly what the man was doing. Perhaps even waving me to a parking space.

He was not. 'You can't park there,' he said, indicating where I'd pulled up. 'There's 20-minute waiting at the far side of the station. You just need to turn around, go back round the one-way system, then, just before the Prince of Wales pub, look out for the arrow.' He did a little snake motion with his hand. 'Hang a right there.'

I pondered this new inconvenience for no more than a second, nodding as I did so, to give the impression that I'd absorbed all his instructions, and would do exactly as he'd said. And then turned around, exited the coach station and parked on a double yellow.

I would not be there long, I reasoned (whether I'd caught up with her or I hadn't), and if anyone in uniform came up and challenged me I was fully prepared to cry, scream or run for it. I was relatively safe, I knew – no way could they get a clamp on the car in less than an hour.

Thankfully, no one did challenge me, and I bolted back into the coach station, which was thoughtfully divided into easy-to-manage sections – local buses on the near side, long-distance coaches on the far side, each with a destination clearly displayed on the front.

I made my way across the various stands, passing ambling shoppers and stepping over various bags and holdalls, till I came to an open-sided booth with a single strip light, in which stood a cold-looking man. Worryingly, there were two empty coach stands adjacent to it.

'Excuse me,' I said. 'I'm looking for the next coach to London.'

'Oh, you've missed that,' he said, and my heart sank to my boots. Then rose again when he added, 'That one left over an hour since. The next one … let me see … twenty to three now. Not too long.' He looked me up and down, presumably in search of signs of luggage. 'Have you pre-booked? Because if you haven't –'

'No, no,' I said, shaking my head. 'I'm meeting someone. Thank you.'

'Off it?' he began, but I'd already hurried away, because if she was here, and I could do nothing more than hope that she was, she would surely get out of the cold and sit in the waiting room.

It was seeing Adrianna without a coat that really shook me. Because it really brought it home to me that, had I been too late, that might have been the end of it. She could disappear out of our lives as abruptly as she'd entered them. Just disappear. Leaving nothing but that battered leather jacket. And perhaps – no, what was I talking about? Almost certainly – almost *certainly* – we would never see or hear of her again. Because we would have no way to trace her. Did we even have a photo of her? Yes, of course, I thought – Tyler had some selfies on his mobile. But that was all. No address, either previous or forwarding, no next of kin to get in touch with, no passport, no nothing. Just a Polish birth certificate that would be no use at all. She would melt into our memories and we would never know what had happened to her. Would forget her even? Not us as a family, but social services, definitely. They barely had a file on her. She'd simply become the girl who never was.

It was sobering, and, seeing her, I felt a jolt of determination. No way was I going to let *that* happen. She was turned half away from me, thankfully, and the doors were pneumatic, so I was able to enter the waiting room silently.

I looked around then, casing the joint like a TV detective, checking out the locations of the two other travellers currently holed up there, and, as far as I could see, there was no exit she could flee from. Satisfied I had her cornered, I approached.

I say approached, but something primal can take over a person sometimes. Particularly when it's a woman. When it's a mother. When it's *me*. It was, therefore, more of a march than a walk, and my tone slightly short of 'calm and measured'.

'Adrianna,' I barked. 'What on earth d'you think you're *doing*?'

Her head snapped back. Her mouth opened. She uttered something like 'Oh!' Then something else, flustered sounding, in Polish.

I plonked myself down on the adjacent red plastic seat. 'Seriously. What were you thinking? What were you – *are* you *doing*?'

'Casey, I am so sorry –' she began. 'You have been so –'

'That's not an answer,' I answered.

'I am sorry –' she began again.

'Adrianna, answer my *question*. What are you *doing* here? Where are you planning on going? London?' She nodded slightly. 'I knew it,' I said. 'And on what exactly? Shirt buttons?'

'Casey, I *am* sorry.' She held her hand up now, clearly determined not to be shushed again. 'I am sorry for making so much trouble for your family. I was going to write to you, I *promise*. I have your address. And I would – *will* – send money. For keeping me. I just have to go now. I have to *work* –'

'Money? For heaven's sake. *Money*?'

I regrouped. Took a breath. 'But why, sweetheart? *Why*? What ridiculous notion have you now got in your brain?'

'I am not ridiculous,' she answered, and there was a spark in her eyes. 'I am too big trouble, and now I have made everything worser. I think and I think and I *know* I cannot stay here. I am too old. Is all too much big imposition.' She stumbled slightly over the word. 'I must not be a scrounger. I must not expect you to keep me and feed me. I must work, and earn money, so I can prove I can be mother –'

'What you must do is stop talking such nonsense, Adrianna,' I huffed. 'Stop it right now this minute!'

She blinked at me, and I realised she'd never seen me so fired up before. But now she would. Oh, yes, now she would. 'You are *not* an imposition, or a scrounger, or a nuisance. Or too old, for that matter. You are a *child*.'

'Casey, I am *16*!'

'Which to me, and the state, for that matter, *is* a child. A minor, if you want to get picky about it. And a vulnerable one at that. Saints alive! You know the word "vulnerable"? That's *you*, Adrianna. God, what's got into you? Where on earth did this nonsense all come from?'

I grabbed her hands, which were clasped in her lap, holding a tissue. Grabbed them none too gently, and then shook them slightly, too. 'Where in the world did you pick up this silly, silly notion that no one can ever be allowed to *help* you? Where did you get this ridiculous idea that you are not *worthy* of anyone's help? Hmm?' I pressed. 'Eh? Great Britain – great people? Wasn't that what you said to me? So let us *help* you, okay? You want to be an "independent Polish girl", then you must stop running away. No more running away, sweetheart, okay? We get you sorted, and we *help* you become that independent Polish girl. Once you are *better*. And we will help you find your baby, I promise.' I squeezed her hand again. 'And in the meantime, you are coming home with me. Jeepers, love, I can't believe we're even *sitting* here!'

I really *couldn't* believe we were sitting there. And attracting the sort of covert attention that public displays of emotion in such places invariably did. Well, it passed the time waiting for coaches, I supposed.

Adrianna said nothing. Mostly because she physically couldn't, having rendered herself mute by the huge, convulsive sobs that had been steadily building since the moment she'd seen me, and which she now seemed powerless to stop.

I reached between her knees for Tyler's backpack. His very old, battered backpack. 'You're under house arrest anyway,' I quipped. 'For stealing this.'

I waved it in front of her as I hauled her to her feet. Which was possibly a misjudgement – no, definitely a misjudgement. Because it just produced another bout of anguished tears.

Which continued all the way out of the coach station and out to the road where, miracle of miracles, I had not got a ticket. I then shovelled her into the passenger seat and tugged on her seatbelt. 'Here you go,' I told her. 'Now, sit and *stay!*' Which at least produced a whisper of a smile.

Then I walked around the boot, opened my own door, slung Tyler's backpack on the back seat and, once belted up myself, gave her my phone.

'I need you to text Mike,' I said, as she began to compose herself.

'And say what?' she asked meekly.

'Hmm …,' I said. 'Let me see … Tell him … yes. Tell him "Elvis *hasn't* left the building".'

We were halfway home before Adrianna stopped sniffing and snivelling, and only then, I suspected, because she'd run out of tissues and wouldn't have dreamt of wiping her nose on her sleeve. Which was a comforting thought. Perhaps I knew her better than I thought I did. Perhaps, actually – and perhaps I would discuss this with Mike later – a lot of what you knew about a person you knew intuitively; knew simply by virtue of a lifetime of being around people, and picking up on all those little non-verbal signals that said so much over and above mere words.

I knew something else, as well. That, like the car, if we wanted to we could park this whole escapade. And, on balance, I felt perhaps we *should* keep this between us. I'd tell Mike, obviously, because he already knew half the story. But did John need to know about this minor blip, really? Because now I'd found Adrianna, that was all it was – a minor blip. A momentary madness in a fraught situation. A world away from a missing 16-year-old.

Not so much John, actually, because John was a level-headed soul, but social services – did they need any of this on their records? Thinking ahead – to the business of Adrianna's baby, and the power they would wield over her – no, they absolutely did not.

'You know,' I said to Adrianna, when we were on the home run to home (and, with a bit of luck, with still a half hour till Tyler rolled in from school), 'I sort of understand why you bolted. It was a gut reaction, wasn't it? You know, once you'd told me everything. You were scared. And I get that. You've been on your own so long now. I completely understand. It's a hard thing, when you're used to having only yourself to rely on – it must feel almost claustrophobic – you know that word?' Adrianna nodded. 'Hard to cope with – that huge loss of control. And I can see where you are coming from, in terms of us looking after you. I can see why you might think it was wrong for you to stay. But you're wrong. We get help, from the government, to do our fostering. An allowance, to make sure you have everything you need. I think it's important you know that.'

She sighed. 'But it *still* feels all wrong. To expect it.'

'Who said you expected it?'

'People,' she answered.

'Oh really?' I pricked my ears up.

'For some people, I am taking money from British children,' she persisted. 'I know this. I understand it is unfair.'

'Who said so?' I countered.

'I can read and I have ears, Casey. I *know* it. I see it in newspapers and the television every day. I saw it in Donna's café that day. I heard what those ladies were saying. They don't think I belong. They never will. And it's not just them, Casey. Other people also say this.'

'In the hospital?'

'That as well, yes.'

'No one there was mean to you, were they?'

'No, not at all. All the nurses. The ladies in the ward with me –'

'You missed a trick there,' I said. 'You could easily have come home with a hand-knitted scarf.'

Adrianna smiled. 'Peggy. That lady, she is called Peggy. She is lovely. And the sister? Sister Skaja? She is so lovely too.'

'Exactly,' I said. 'You know, you'll find most people *are*. And another thing. When you worry about money, think about this. That for every girl like you – and you are thankfully a rarity – there are dozens, if not hundreds, of hard-working Poles. Who all pay their taxes, and all make a contribution, and if they thought a tiny part of that – because it *is* a tiny part – was going towards helping you make a good, productive life, then what do you think they would say? They'd say go for it. Because it's not about now – it's about what you will contribute in the *future*. Which will be *so* much.' I sniffed. 'Now you're getting *me* going. Enough. So let's say no more about it, okay?'

'Okay,' Adrianna said. 'I know I am stupid. I cannot believe I have been so stupid for so *long*. To tell you such nonsense. To lie …'

'Not stupid,' I told her. 'You were frightened when you came to us. I understand that. You might have it wrong about immigrants and detention centres – you definitely *do* have it wrong about immigrants and detention centres, as it happens. But if you'd told them your real age when you went to social services, you're right – you might not have been sent to us. Or, indeed, to *any* foster family. You might well have been put in lodgings.'

'Lodgings? Are they like squats?'

'Yes, sometimes,' I said. All too often, I thought – it was a fine line. 'Like you might have ended up back in if you'd got on that flipping coach. A room in a grotty house some-where. With other vulnerable people. No family. No friends.'

'Oh, Casey,' she said, swivelling in her seat. 'How sad I am to have lied to you for so long. I have lain there in my hospital bed, wide awake, so much. *So* much. I am so sorry for that. And now all this, too … I feel terrible.'

157

I shot her a look. 'Don't start again. That's all done with, okay? No more discussion.'

She shook her head. 'I hate to think of you all thinking I have deceived you. And Tyler. I feel so awful … he … he will be so upset …'

She didn't need to finish. We both knew what she meant as far as Tyler was concerned. 'Listen, about Tyler,' I said, as we turned into our street. 'We haven't told him about the baby. Or your age, for that matter. He just knows that you were ill and are now better. We thought you might like to have the opportunity to tell him yourself. I think it would be better coming from you. If you feel able to … what with everything.' I tutted. 'Specially now you tried to run away with his favourite backpack. He'd have been inconsolable …' I laughed. Adrianna did as well.

'Oh, Casey,' she said, and, though I was busy parallel parking, I could still hear the catch in her throat. 'I am so happy that you have done that. I shall do it. I shall explain. And it will be okay, I know. I promise. Tyler is my *ziom*.'

'I know what *ziom* means,' I said, hoping she was right about that. 'Tyler told me, just before you came to us.'

'He is getting good with his Polish,' she said. 'He is a lovely, lovely boy.'

Boy, I thought. Of all the ways she could describe him. The very last word Tyler would want to have affixed to him. In this circumstance, anyway. Poor Tyler.

'He is,' I said. 'We love him very much.'

She turned her head. 'And you are a lovely mum,' she said. I cleared my throat. We were *definitely* going to have to knock this on the head. 'No more running away,' she promised. 'I have learned now. I have learned from *you*,' she said, 'very much. And now,' she finished, and the relief in her voice was unmistakable, 'I am going to be a lovely mum to my own boy.'

'Of course you are,' I said as I switched off the ignition. And was just taking my belt off when she started contorting her body.

'What on earth are you doing?' I asked her, as she started undoing her skinny jeans.

She grunted as she wriggled them down and her jumper up and started rummaging around in the tights she had on under them. 'I have something to give you,' she said, scrabbling her hands behind her back. 'Now,' she said. 'Now. It is important.'

'Can't it wait?' I said, watching her struggle with her various layers of clothing.

'No, I must do this now. To prove to you.'

'If you say so,' I said, continuing to watch, mystified, till at last I heard her say, 'Ah. Now I have it.' Upon which she slid something long and flat from round her middle. Only when she placed it in my hands did I see what it was. A slim, canvas, flesh-coloured money belt. Ah, I thought, feeling the warmth from it. Ah, now I *see*.

'There is £40, I think,' she said. 'You and Mike. You must have this. This was my fund … to escape. If I needed to.' She smiled shyly. 'I wore it always. So you might want to wash it.'

Chapter 13

Even if she'd been exposed to British radio comedy, which she probably hadn't, Adrianna was obviously too young to know anything about the iconic series called *The Glums*. Ditto Tyler, of course. But there was no getting away from it. After all the drama – and relief – that came with Adrianna's confession, it was now like we were living in an episode of it.

I'd been very happy to step back when it came to Adrianna telling Tyler that, actually, she was not what she had seemed. And she'd been equally anxious to address the problem right away. They'd holed themselves up, not long after he got home from school that afternoon, and when they emerged – Adrianna thoughtful-looking, Tyler a little pale – I didn't mention their conversation, and neither did they. I just dished up the tea, with a side order of near-unbroken, bland, idle chit-chat, and trusted my instincts that it would all soon blow over. Because, however hard Ty had seemed to fall for Adrianna, I had a feeling there was a part of him that had always practised self-protection, knowing that, ultimately, she would move on.

Time would tell. But I still had an equally pressing problem to deal with. That, having reassured her on all fronts as a matter of course when bringing her home again, I still had to make clear that there were difficult times ahead; that her belief that getting her baby back would be relatively simple was one that needed tempering with some cool, rational facts.

I cursed whoever put the idea into her head in the first place. Well, would have, were the target that clear. It seemed she'd had multiple conversations, with multiple fellow patients over the weekend, all of whom, it seemed, had contributed to her belief that there were some things that were almost woven into the fabric of the Union flag; that a mother and her child should always be together – that she and the baby would be united, because that was the *right* way.

'And I have been thinking,' she told me, while helping with the housework on the Wednesday morning – she really *was* something of a little domestic fairy, it turned out, and extremely anxious to make herself useful. 'I can get a job. And work hard. And will be able to support him. It is not true that I am not allowed to work here legally, and I have looked online' – she still had the freedom of Tyler's laptop when he was at school – 'and there are many jobs for cleaners, and waitresses, and shop girls. I think I will be okay to get a good job with good pay. I have already made some notes about places to apply.'

Much as I applauded her work ethic – which was, indeed, laudable – at the same time I felt my spirits sink. There was no point in putting the conversation off further. No point in waiting, as I had been, till John came round for the formal meeting. There was a theme building. That it was more a case of 'when', rather than 'if'. And while I still believed that the 'when' part would eventually happen, there seemed increasingly to be a mismatch in our ideas about how soon that 'when' was going to be. 'Sweetheart,' I said, 'you know what? I think we need to sit down and discuss all this properly.'

'Properly?' she asked, her dark brows coming together.

'Properly,' I repeated. 'So. To the kitchen.'

Well, the conservatory, ultimately, once I was armed with a coffee and Adrianna with the cranberry juice she seemed to down by the litre.

I liked our conservatory. It was what psychologists would have probably called a 'good space'. It looked out onto a garden that, although in large part still in its winter slumber, offered plenty of colour; the zingy spring green of well-watered grass and the cheerful yellows of the now blooming daffodils. It also meant we could sit, very companionably, on our old rattan sofa, looking out onto the garden rather than facing each other, which I'd long learned made for less confrontational conversations and, with less eye contact, made anxious kids more inclined to open up.

And there I explained to Adrianna, slowly and calmly, about all the hoops, as John put it, that she might still have to jump through. That it was not simply a case of them delivering her baby to us, but instead, now the state had effectively become her baby's parent, of her having to prove that they could absolutely trust that handing him back to her would be the right thing to do.

'Which is why,' I impressed upon her (and as forcefully as possible), 'you did the right thing in coming home with me on Monday, rather than running away again.'

All this she seemed to take in. Well, ostensibly she did, anyway, fully accepting that because of what she'd done – giving birth in a toilet, not seeking medical care, not approaching the authorities sooner – it could be argued that she didn't have his best interests at heart *then*, even though – as *I* knew – she actually did. She also accepted that, in being thorough, the authorities were doing the right thing as well. 'Doing right by your *child*, Adrianna,' I pointed out, 'just as you had trusted that they would.'

And she was grateful – so grateful – that he was being so well cared for.

But the gulf between her imaginings and the reality was revealed nevertheless, when she turned to me and asked, 'How long must I wait, then? Not weeks? Some months? As long as that?'

I took her hand and gripped it. 'Sweetheart, look, this is only a worst-case scenario, okay? You know what that is?' She nodded. 'So what I'm about to tell you is the *longest* time, as far as I know, anyway. It could be less. But I have to tell you, because I want you to understand and prepare for it, that it will probably take longer than that. Perhaps as long as two years.'

The silence mushroomed and bellowed, the shock written plainly on her face. And, once she took it in, there was absolutely no consoling her. No comforting. No 'there, there'-ing. She was horrified. Astounded. Appalled. 'It might be nowhere as long,' I kept saying, though I knew it was to deaf ears. 'But these things take *time*, sweetheart. A lot of time. because of what I've already said. You are young. You have been through a very great deal. You will recover from it all –'

'I am *already* recovered!'

'From the *mental* scars, Adrianna. The trauma. The abuse. The displacement from your *home*.'

'I *have* no home!' she cried. 'Only here. Only *here*.' Her expression changed suddenly, and I realised something else must have occurred to her.

'I have to go. I *should* have gone. I have to make a home. I have to go to lodgings. I have to live in a room and get a job. I must go.'

I shook my head. 'No, no, *no*,' I said. 'You *don't* have to go. Not in the short term. Of course you don't. Let's have no more of that talk, please! Yes, in time you do – and I'm sure you will want to, in any case. If you're going to make a life for your baby, then, yes, of *course* you will have to prove that you can manage on your own. That you can support yourself *and* a baby. That's how you will get him back. But all of that will take time …'

'And till then? He doesn't know me? I am a stranger? He loves his foster mummy? He does not want to come to me?'

She was so bright. And, perhaps because of that, even more inconsolable. 'It won't be *like* that,' I said, my voice growing firmer, as I took in how much she needed purpose and strength. 'You will work hard to make sure you can give him a home with *you*. And while you are doing that, you will see him. You will see him regularly, Adrianna. And then you will have him back again, all to yourself. And, don't forget, he'll still be so young, even then. And as he grows he will forget. How much do you remember about your first two years? Anything?'

'But it isn't that!' She tapped her temple. 'It is the damage inside *here*!'

'Adrianna, that is not going to happen! He won't remember anything of the time when he was in care, either consciously, or' – I tapped my own head – 'in *here*. Only that he was always, *always* loved. That's what matters. Trust me, that's what matters.'

She fell against me sobbing, and, thinking of Tyler's start in life, I could have cried too. 'It hurts so much,' Adrianna cried. 'So much.'

'I know,' I said. 'Shhh … come on, chin up. You can do this. Remember, your baby is safe and well and happy. He does *not* hurt. As a mother, let that give you strength.'

'And to forget.'

'To forget?'

'For me. For *my* life. How much I would like to be able to forget. Some chemical I could take – drug –' She raised a finger to her temple. 'And then – kapow – it's all gone. All the bad. Just the good left. My father.' Almost a whisper now. 'I would like that so much.'

It was the first time she'd really shared any of the emotion about what had happened to her. And being a bright girl, she'd got right to the heart of it, too. Rub it out. Take it away. Kapow. All gone.

If only it could really be that simple.

Back in the present, the next few days saw the emotional temperature in the Watson household move from *The Glums* to a version of *Within These Walls*. Though she tried her best to keep smiling, it was like watching a plant wilt. Nothing I could say seemed to lift Adrianna's spirits. If she had looked pale and drained before, she now walked around as if the very life had been sucked out of her.

It was a natural reaction. I knew this. She was pining for her baby and there was nothing anyone could do to stop that happening. I understood the mechanism, too. She'd spent the best part of three months now running on adrenalin. Always looking over her shoulder, always worrying that she might be found out. But as soon as she had been, it was as if a dam had opened – adrenalin whooshing out, and the reality flooding in; the baby that she had carried for nine months was gone, and although she could concede that she had done what she thought was best for him, she now bitterly regretted giving him up.

'You know, Casey,' she said the following Friday afternoon. 'In my head I named him. I named him Jakob.'

It was said out of the blue, while I was reading the paper.

'What?' I said, not having quite heard her the first time.

'My boy,' she continued. She was at the sink, washing up our lunch things. Staring out of the window. 'In my head he was Jakob. And they do not know.' She turned around. 'Casey, you know, I once saw a movie where a lady gave up her baby girl, and she wrote the baby's name on a label and pinned it to her vest. So her new parents knew what to call her. What her name was. I should have done that. Oh, how I wish I had done that.'

It was such a sad thing to say, and I knew she wasn't expecting an answer. It was simply another reason for her sadness; another regret.

I went to the sink and hugged her. 'Darling, *please* don't upset yourself like this. It won't help you. Yes, you're right, he will have another name; a name you didn't give him. They will have had to do that, of *course*. But you know, you have to remember that what you did, you did *for* him. You showed incredible maternal love in giving him away. Beside that ... well, does a name matter so much? And, in time, there's no reason why you can't add the name Jakob. Make it his middle name, perhaps.'

The thought seemed to console her. 'I had not thought of that.'

'Well, there you are. Something nice to think about, eh? To help keep you strong. Because you'll need to be, sweetheart. So we need less regret, okay? And to see more of that independent Polish girl! Well,' I added, 'not *too* much.'

She knew what I meant, and I felt her smiling against my shoulder. 'I will try, Casey. I promise. For my little Something Jakob.'

It was so hard for her, though. How could it not be? I knew because we'd been here before with another girl we'd fostered, Emma. A girl who'd come to us with her new-born but had him taken away, so I knew full well how much pain Adrianna must be in. Especially knowing he was so far away. Not a million miles away, true, but a long way out of reach, and I hoped there might be some chance of John speaking to the authorities and persuading them to have him moved closer. That would at least be a start.

But *only* a start. There was a long way to go. The next step would be the huge task of making the decision about whether Adrianna might actually be allowed to have her baby back. Without that, there would *be* no next steps.

But I knew I mustn't get too ahead of myself. That was in the future. Right now I had a broken 16-year-old to deal with, and I was at something of a loss.

Thank heavens for Tyler, then, who burst into the kitchen at precisely that moment and though momentarily dumbstruck to see Adrianna crying, soon rallied, in that endearing can-do way he had.

She sprang away from me, grabbed a sheet of kitchen roll to wipe her eyes with and, seemingly as anxious as Tyler to normalise things, said, 'You have a good day at school? Oh, and guess what? I have finished the book!'

I might be fanciful, but I reckoned all was well on the Tyler front. However he had rationalised this new reality since that initial period of awkwardness, I'd have said their relationship had become even closer. I definitely think he had a new level of respect for Adrianna.

He threw his school bag on the floor. 'Then we'll have to choose you a new one. Though it's a hard act to follow. And, yeah, was all right. But, hey, listen.'

Adrianna nodded and sat down at the kitchen table. 'Of course,' she said, just as I said, 'To what?'

'Well,' Tyler started, 'I had this idea. I watched this episode of *CSI* last night, and it was all about this lady who left her baby on a bus to be looked after by the lady who she left it by.'

I digested this, then looked at Tyler in horror. What was he *thinking*? But before I could stop him, he carried on.

'Anyway, the lady took the baby to the police and left it there, but eventually the real mum came forward and confessed, and in the end she got the baby back and they didn't throw her in jail, because that's, like, an offence you know? Abandonment? I didn't know that.'

I was torn between holding my breath and rugby tackling him. What on earth had possessed him to tell her such a tale? Still, it had been said now, and there was obviously no way of unsaying it. So all I could do was wait for Adrianna's reaction.

Which was typically understated and sensible. 'Is this true, Casey?' she asked me. 'Did I do an offence?'

I gave Tyler one of my very specific looks. 'Tyler, what are you thinking?' I asked him, trying to match Adrianna's composure. 'Giving Adrianna something *else* to worry about! It was just a TV show. And, no, Adrianna, I'm not sure it is. Not in your circumstances. And anyway, the show's set in America.'

Tyler looked indignant. 'Hang on! I didn't get to my idea yet!'

'You have an idea?' I asked him, wondering what was going to come next.

'Of course! I'm not stupid! It's a very sensible idea. If the police come asking questions, she just needs to tell them she wasn't in her right mind. Just like the woman did. And you probably weren't in your right mind anyway, were you?'

'No, I wasn't,' Adrianna agreed, with feeling.

'See?' Tyler said to me. 'Sorted. Specially as she's fine now. They can't pin a thing on her.'

Adrianna looked at me quizzically. 'Is this right?' she asked.

'Well, yes,' I said. 'It is. Not that I was expecting the boys in blue to be arresting you anytime soon *in the first place*,' I stressed, giving Tyler another pointed look. 'But yes, it's true. Although you were doing the very best for your baby, at the time, you *weren't* well after having him, and not in a fit state to think straight. So no, I don't think you need worry about any of that.'

To my surprise I watched her then grin at Tyler. 'But if they do,' she said, 'I now know the drill. I tell them I was cuckoo and ga-ga then. Sweet!'

At which they both burst out laughing, like any normal,

run-of-the-mill, everyday teenagers would. So perhaps he hadn't been so stupid after all.

Now we just needed John to come and wave his magic wand.

Chapter 14

I hadn't seriously imagined that Adrianna would be charged with anything, because we were living in the twenty-first century, not the twelfth, and, besides, she hadn't abandoned her child anyway. Far from it. She'd done the responsible thing in an appalling situation and had left him in a safe place, to be taken care of by the authorities.

And it was so easy to forget, given her unfailing self-possession, just what an appalling situation it really was. She'd been forced to run away from home (and that in itself must have been harrowing enough), only to fall victim to a predatory male intent on trafficking her, becoming his – and his gang's – virtual prisoner, and then finding the wherewithal to run away a second time, only to find out she was pregnant with his child.

Really, it was a miracle that she wasn't in total meltdown – a seething cauldron of deep-rooted psychological issues; the proverbial, not to mention, profoundly damaged, troubled young person with whom psychologists would 'have a field day'.

I tried not to think about it, but a part of me wondered where down the line all this *was* going to manifest itself. Because how could it not affect her at a fundamental level, to have been through so much hurt and anguish so young? It seemed impossible that it wouldn't in some way.

Trafficked. I tried to blot the word out, very consciously. Because it had just become altogether too ubiquitous. And when words become that common they often lose their power. 'Oh, she's been trafficked' hasn't half the emotional power of 'She's been groomed and then kidnapped and then held a virtual prisoner and forced to perform sex acts on strangers.'

Which was why I was actually pleased to hear John was bringing the police round. Yes, it might traumatise Adrianna initially, but it was very welcome evidence that they were going to take what had happened to her very seriously.

That said, it didn't make for restful sleep. And when I was still tossing and turning at twenty to six the next morning, I gave up, and got up and showered.

It took a good ten minutes under the showerhead to get me going, during which time I speculated – pretty pointlessly – on what might happen next. Since John had phoned I had spent half the time assuring Adrianna that everything would be fine and that we could just take each day as it came, and the other half playing out scenarios in my head – none of which had even remotely happy endings.

It had been the word 'urgent' that had made me prick up my ears. 'We'd like to meet tomorrow, if you can do it,' he'd said. 'That's the best time for the police.'

It had been the first time he'd mentioned that they'd wanted to interview Adrianna and it had hit me that maybe I'd been wrong. Despite my many assurances, I'd nevertheless done a bit of googling and had stumbled upon a report of a trafficked girl who'd been brought into the country illegally, and who went to the authorities and rather than being helped – or, according to the report, even believed – she *had* been put in a detention centre. But the girl in question had come from Somalia, which made the situation different. Somalia was not part of the EU and, without a visa, she had fallen victim to the business of immigration 'procedures' – which, in this case, involved popping her in the detention centre, out of the way, and investigating what had happened to her from there.

This absolutely didn't apply to Adrianna. As she too had come in illegally and would be unable to produce a passport, in theory, yes, she could be contravening some identity-related law. But as both a victim of a crime and a certified EU national (thank heavens for her birth certificate), on what basis could they even think of charging her with anything?

But what did I know? Seriously? Almost nothing. 'She isn't going to get in trouble, is she?' I asked him, Tyler's pronouncements ringing in my ears.

'Oh, I don't think so,' John said. 'Not for a moment. But they do want to question Adrianna about the paternity of the baby. They want to know more about the man she came into the UK with, apparently, so they know what, if any, action to take.'

'If?' I replied. 'There's even an if about it?'

'I don't think so,' he said again. 'But the theory and the reality might be poles apart – if you'll excuse the pun. These characters are probably as slippery as eels, don't you think? I guess it will depend on how many man hours they can devote to the problem, won't it?'

He had a point. Foreign pimps running foreign girls; would it really be a priority? There was enough 'home-grown' crime, with similarly 'home-grown' victims, to keep the police busy for for ever and a day. But they *were* investigating, at least at this point, which had to be a good thing. I said so.

'Plus it's a great opportunity for Adrianna to meet her social worker,' John went on.

'So you've found one? Fantastic. That was quick.'

'Wasn't difficult. Not now we don't need one who speaks Polish. She's been allocated Jasmine Erskine. Kids call her Jazz. She's nice. Adrianna will like her. Have you come across her before at all? I couldn't remember.'

'I don't believe I have,' I said. 'Oh, but I'm so glad we have someone on board now. This whole police business is going to unsettle Adrianna, I know. She's not said as much, but I'm pretty sure she is going to be terrified at the prospect of helping them with their enquiries. I really think she is scared of those men, and what they might do to her.'

'Of course,' John agreed. 'I totally understand that. But, at the same time, her co-operation will go a long way towards strengthening her case re the little one, won't it?'

He made a very important point. It was exactly the sort of thing that would prove her to be a helpful, honest citizen. 'You're right. Any news about that, by the way?'

'Well, actually, there is a bit of a silver lining here,' he said. 'I was going to wait until I had more specific details before telling you, but I'm guessing you'll need a bit of a carrot to tempt Adrianna into co-operating tomorrow, so maybe you can at least share a bit of this.'

John went on to tell me about the exciting developments that had been going on behind the scenes. The family that had been given temporary care of Adrianna's baby had – amazingly – already been traced and interviewed. So that part of it really had been 'simples'! They had been given chapter and verse about Adrianna, too; put in the picture about the circumstances of the baby's birth, and also asked if it might be possible for Adrianna, together with a social worker, to go to London to meet them and be introduced again to her child.

This was all very exciting, of course, and just the thing to lift Adrianna's spirits. But John was right that I should only share this information with caution; I mustn't make a big deal of it, in case it all came to nothing. It would be a long road, and one that had no definite destination. Every time she saw her baby – assuming regular contact was, as we hoped, agreed – she would be assessed as to her suitability to take sole responsibility for him again. Which was not a decision any council would – or should – ever take lightly.

And in this case, though initially completely happy to say yes, the couple had apparently backtracked just a little, asking for a bit more time so they could run things past their own social worker. So, even though John was still positive, you never knew. And despite the fact that I wouldn't say anything to Adrianna unless I thought I had to, there was always the possibility that the family would make a case for holding on to him; even in the longer term adopting him. There were many couples out there, after all, who were desperate to adopt a newborn child – a situation only exacerbated because there were so few around.

So I was very mindful, overall, of the potential potholes along the road. Adrianna, however, had no such emotional regulator. Just the knowledge that her baby had been found and there was a potential visit on the table was enough to create another 360 degree turnaround in her mood; try as she might, she simply couldn't keep a level head about it.

I had to keep reminding myself – she was only 16. A time of hormones in torrents at the best of times. She couldn't see beyond seeing him, and her all-will-be-well gauge was set to max.

She was also hyper and sleepless, like me.

'Good morning, Casey!' she greeted me, when I appeared down in the kitchen. 'Your favourite beverage,' she said, thrusting a mug of coffee at me. 'I heard you in the shower,' she explained, obviously noting my consternation. 'And I do toast for you, also. You sit.'

'You're up very early,' I said as she pulled out a chair for me. 'And go on, then,' I added, sitting down. 'I'll have a piece of toast.'

'I think I was bitten by those bed bugs Tyler explained to me,' she said as she bustled around the kitchen, 'and I am just *so* excited for our meeting, I could not sleep a wink. When do you think it will happen? Will John know? Oh, I cannot wait to see Jakob …' She immediately corrected herself. I mean my baby Something Jakob. I am very nervous to find out what's his name.'

'Come sit down,' I said, patting the seat beside me. 'And *calm* down. Before you make yourself ill again.'

'I will, I will,' she sang, peering into the toaster as she did so. 'We must both eat. I understand. And I will sit down.'

She duly came across and joined me with the toast and her tea. 'You know,' she said, unscrewing the jam jar, 'I am so tense. Like a spring. I think I must also have the bed bugs in my pants.'

I couldn't help laughing. And also choking on my coffee. Tyler was obviously having his own field day with her. He was milking it, for sure. 'No, darling,' I explained. 'That's not quite how it works. It's "Night, night, sleep tight, don't let the bed bugs bite" when you go to *sleep*. And it's "ants in your pants" when you are jumpy and nervous. Two completely different sayings.'

'That hardest bit of English is the bits that aren't written. I remember my father telling me that. And he was right.'

'You must miss him terribly,' I said, watching for her reaction over my mug.

'I do,' she said simply. 'I will miss him all my life. But he's here.' She touched her chest. 'And he will live on in Jakob. That was his name, you know. Jakob.'

Not the name on the birth certificate I'd seen. I said so.

She shook her head. 'Not on paper. He was named for his father – my grandfather. Which caused great confusion when he was young,' she explained. 'So, for the family, always Jakob. Or "Jakobbbbbbbbb!" so my gran said. Anyway,' she finished, finally putting jam on her toast, 'today I have ants in my pants.'

I reached across to put my hand on her shoulder. 'Sweetheart, remember what I told you? You must remember that today is about lots of different things, as well as *perhaps* arranging a meeting to see your baby. You understand that, don't you?'

Adrianna nodded. 'Casey, I know. Please don't worry. It's about him. And the other men, and the customers, too. I understand that. Don't you worry. I will not let you down.'

'I never thought you would for a moment,' I reassured her. 'I don't think you could let me down if you tried. And it will be a good meeting – after this, everything will start to get better. You'll meet your social worker, Jazz – well, or Jasmine, if you prefer. And –'

'She's nice, Jasmine? You said you don't know her. Do you trust her?'

'Trust her? Of course I do. She is there to help you, I told you. Why would you ask?'

Adrianna seemed reluctant to speak. But then leaned in towards me. 'I wasn't sure whether to speak, but I have been very anxious. Social workers take babies. I know this. My friends in London –'

'Oh, Adrianna …'

'No, really, Casey. *Often*. My friends in London, two of them have babies which were taken away from them. Both times by social workers …'

I didn't doubt it. I could all too easily imagine the scenario. The usual tragic cocktail of runaways, teen pregnancies, drug abuse, homelessness. So where did you start? Some lives started appallingly and simply became worse, the future already pre-determined by the past.

'You're right,' I said. What was the point in saying anything different? 'That does sometimes happen. But only *ever* to protect the child. They would never remove a baby, or an older child, from a mother who didn't have problems. And I even if they did, they would do all in their power to help solve it, because taking a child from its parent is the very *last* thing they want to do. *Honestly*. No one wants that to happen, Adrianna, ever. So you must learn to trust these people, sweetie. To understand what they are there for. They really do want to help and Jazz is there to help you. She is your advocate. By your side. Coming round especially for *you*.'

She seemed to digest this, along with her toast. 'And with the police? She is there to help me if the police want to do mug shots and fingerprints? And DNA tests?'

'Now you really are running away with yourself, sweetheart,' I said, as I got up. 'Yes, you might have to provide DNA – that's completely normal these days. For many reasons, including proving you're the baby's mother. But as for the rest, I think you need not believe *quite* so much of what Tyler gets from *CSI* ...'

I also made a mental note to try to get Tyler interested in something a tad less 'criminal mayhem'. In fact, a lot less. My box sets of *Downton Abbey*, perhaps.

Chapter 15

Seeing the cars pull up outside took the wind out of Adrianna's sails. Up to now she'd been surfing a wave of optimism, and, conscious that my job was to try to keep her calm and centred, I'd been at pains – well, as far as was possible, given the need to manage her expectations – not to be the one to tip her off her surfboard.

We'd prepared together, her laying out the obligatory plate of biscuits, while I got the obligatory 'best' china out. These were the things that had become rituals since Mike and I had started fostering. Formal meetings with professionals had become routine now; just another regular aspect of our job. But I still treated them just as I had from the very first time we were obliged to host one, and the butterflies in my stomach had taken such agitated flight.

These days, I wondered quite what all the fuss had been about. Why I used to get so stressed about having all these important people in our house. Why I'd worried so much about making the 'right' impression – after all, what was the right impression anyway? We were foster carers, for goodness' sake. Not there to fly the flag for *Homes & Gardens*. What did it matter if I served coffee in mugs rather than cups, or that my sofa arms were possibly a little frayed? But the class divide never manifested itself quite so clearly as when strangers were in your home who might not be from your class. Strangers who might look at how you lived and judge you. Perhaps the class system in Britain would never truly go away. But what nonsense. We would be judged on what we did, not on our crockery. Even so, out it all came.

And it was thinking about all this that reminded me, as it usually did, of the importance of seeing proceedings through the eyes of a traumatised, frightened child. A child who might already be with us and be having some aspect of their eventual fate discussed or, as was so often the case, a child for whom we were complete strangers and for whom the whole business must be so much more terrifying.

I even smiled to myself as I looked at the refreshments; the shiny-foil-wrapped biscuits I always set out as a matter of course now, their jewel colours inviting and beguiling. Where the posh cups and saucers said 'we are your equals', the pretty biscuits said 'we are your friends'. I hoped Adrianna would feel among friends today.

Following Adrianna's alert, I left the dining table and joined her at the window, where she was silently observing the occupants climbing out of the two cars parked out front. I had no idea what logistics had brought them here together – had John driven to the police station and led the police officers here in convoy? Or was their arrival together simply the manifestation of split-second timing? Either way, both sets of car doors closed again in synchrony – the first having disgorged John and, presumably, Jasmine, and the second, which wasn't a marked police car but could be nothing else, two other people, who were presumably plain-clothed police officers, one female, one male.

'I'm a little bit scared now,' Adrianna whispered.

I squeezed her hand. 'Don't be. You're not in trouble, and you have nothing to fear.'

'That is the social worker?' she whispered again. 'The one with the pink fluffy jacket?'

'I think so,' I said, watching the woman follow John up the path, ahead of the police officers. 'She looks nice, doesn't she?'

Adrianna nodded. 'And she is young. I thought she would be older. I thought social workers would be always older.'

'Oh no, not at all,' I said. 'They come in all shapes and sizes. Anyway, come on. The doorbell's going to go .... right about *now*.'

Which it did. She followed me out into the hall.

Social workers did indeed come in all shapes and sizes. And colours, and ages, and political affiliations, and degrees of devotion to their charges and their jobs. As I was sure applied in all walks of life. And both in my time as a foster

carer and, before that, as a school behaviour manager, I had
come across, and worked with, a lot.

Which at least gave me a modicum of instinct about
them and, on opening the front door and meeting Jasmine's
eye, my instinct was that John had chosen very well.

Well, if 'chosen' was the right word, which, a lot of the
time it wasn't, because in an overstretched service with an
always-growing workload, who you 'got' was decided as
much on expediency as anything, and was often more a case
of Hobson's choice. But I recalled John saying that there
had been an element of choice involved with this one – and
that, given that there was one, he'd pressed for someone
female and young, in the cause of getting the most out of
Adrianna.

I agreed with him. Given what had happened to her,
both in Poland and in Britain – not to mention her encoun-
ter with the grumpy male interpreter – I reckoned a woman
would be the best bet. It was going to be hard enough to
encourage her to put her trust in a stranger, and if that
stranger was male, even more so.

Jasmine also had the look of a woman with a bit of steel
in her. Which is difficult to describe, but always easy to
spot. It was there in the pink coat, which was nothing short
of shockingly exuberant, and in the way she immediately
made her focus Adrianna, even as she cowered very slightly
behind me. It was there in the way she held her laptop case,
the way she held herself generally. It said 'I'm here, and I've
got your back and I relish the opportunity.' I suspected
(and, again, I have no idea why, quite) that despite her

relative youth – perhaps mid- to late twenties? – that she was probably also a mum.

'Hello!' I said brightly. 'Come on in out of the cold, everyone. That's the way,' I added as each of them passed me with the usual nod and smile. 'Straight into the living room. Adrianna will show you and take your coats.'

John was last, having ushered the two police officers in ahead of him. 'All well?' he asked.

'Yup,' I said. 'Any more news on anything?'

'A little. All positive,' he said. 'So far.'

And the meeting began positively as well. Despite Adrianna's earlier anxiety, she showed admirable composure. Forget 14, or 16 – her demeanour betrayed her years. It was so easy to forget that she *was* still a child. Or, if your definition, more accurately, be that she was actually now a minor, that she had very much been a child when her world had imploded.

Seated beside me, she listened carefully as the female officer explained who they were and what steps they were going to take next. She was a detective sergeant – hence the plain clothes – and explained that she and her colleague, who was a detective constable, were attached to the vice squad, had travelled a long way to see her and were keen to hear as much as she could tell them about the characters she'd escaped from the previous year.

Though not, it seemed, right now this very minute. 'We're mainly here at this stage,' she said, 'to reassure you, Adrianna. That you're not going to be charged with anything, because you're not guilty of any crime. As you know, everything you've told your foster mum has already been corroborated and we're completely happy that under the circumstances you did exactly the right thing.'

'*Dzieki*,' Adrianna said, inclining her head. 'Sorry – *thank* you. I am very, very much relieved.'

'I'm glad to hear that,' said the lady officer. 'And that you're going to see your baby. And that you've agreed to try to help us if you can.'

'Which is very much the case,' John said. 'Adrianna's very keen to do that, aren't you, Adrianna?'

'Very keen,' Adrianna agreed politely.

Though rather less keen, I reckoned, once they explained what kind of thing that help would entail, which included a visit or two to the local police station – though they used the term Victim Support Unit, often – both to make a formal statement detailing her experiences and her escape, and, if she was willing (and this was the heart of the matter), to spend some time looking at mug shots on their computer database to see if there were any faces she recognised.

'Is that likely?' John asked the male officer, who'd been explaining that part.

He nodded. 'We're optimistic,' he replied. 'Now we know the city we're talking about, we can narrow it down a lot. And as we already have a wide-ranging investigation ongoing, there's every chance we'll be able to put anything Adrianna here can tell us to good use.'

The yin and yang of life, I thought, taking in Adrianna's expression. Calculating though it might seem, there was a necessary trade-off in the mix. And Adrianna knew that too, so, though she'd been previously 'unsure' about any of the details of her experience as a 'modern-day slave' (as they'd put it), she had, since the prospect of getting Jakob back was becoming real, begun remembering more.

And after a good bit of work on Tyler's part, much of it spent with Adrianna on Google Earth, we had been able to establish where she'd been during her first months in the UK, both in terms of city and probable district. And something else – that the young man who'd befriended her in Poland was, in all probability, English. Which was both a shock – a trafficking tourist? – and a plus point. If it was a British gang – as it seemed – there was a good chance the police were already on their tail. And (this shouldn't matter, but I knew how the world worked, so imagined it probably did) it also meant that Adrianna's baby had a British father.

And now Adrianna would have to come good on the next level of detail – the actual identities of the men who were prostituting her. I watched her blanch.

'But if I see a man I know,' she asked, 'what then? Will I have to stand in court where they could see me?'

Both police officers were quick to shake their heads. 'Absolutely not,' the detective sergeant said, 'not unless it's absolutely necessary. And if it did turn out that you were required to give evidence against anyone, you could do so via a video link.'

She glanced at me anxiously. 'That means you wouldn't actually have to be present in court,' I reassured her. 'In cases where there is a risk to the victim,' I went on, glancing at both the officers for corroboration, 'then I think your identity can be kept secret, so you are safe. But, honestly, love, please don't stress yourself about that now. This is all just hypothetical.' I saw the confusion in her eyes and regrouped. 'As in something that isn't definitely going to happen. That's *unlikely* to happen. It's more a question of you helping the police build more of a picture.'

'But they would kill me,' she said, her voice rising slightly, her chin jutting. 'You know this?' She glanced from one officer to the other. 'You know these men? If they find me, they will kill me.'

Sadly, I knew she wasn't being melodramatic. Tyler hadn't been the only one on Google in the last couple of days. Traffickers treating kidnapped girls like animals, beating them, half starving them and making them service (where the word 'service' meant things that were extremely difficult to read, let alone think about) multiple paying clients, often a dozen or so times a day. I could only hope that when Adrianna said she'd got away before things became unbearable she had been telling me the truth. I also knew, because the testimonies were out there, and in spades, that girls who'd been trafficked *did* get killed. And being here illegally, without passports, with family and loved ones so far away, they could be easily disposed of as well.

John, on the other side of me, touched my arm. Silent tears were rolling down Adrianna's cheeks now. 'Oh, sweetheart,' I said, curling an arm around her and pulling her close. 'Shh, now. It's okay.'

She shook her head. 'I am okay. I will help. I am just thinking … That is all. There are other girls. I *must* help. I have trust I will be safe.'

Jasmine had spoken little up to this point. Having formally introduced herself – mostly to me and Adrianna, because it seemed she was already on first-name terms with the two officers – she had mostly just nodded affirmatives and made the odd note on the A4 pad in front of her. But now she reached across the table to throw Adrianna a packet of tissues she'd evidently whipped from her case. 'Here you go, Adrianna,' she said. 'Have a blow on one of those. And you're right to have trust. Take it from me, you can *absolutely* trust these guys, okay? You're being incredibly brave just agreeing to be here. And, you know, those other girls – well, it doesn't need saying, does it?' Adrianna shook her head as she extracted a tissue from the packet. 'You're doing the right thing. And you *will* be kept safe, okay?'

As words, they were just platitudes, really. In reality, no one could give Adrianna that absolute assurance, and even if she moved far, far away, she might well be looking over her shoulder for the rest of her life, whether she was instrumental in getting them convicted or not. All the while these men existed, they would haunt her.

But there was something about the way Jasmine spoke that inspired confidence in me. Something about the way she just exuded commitment. That sense that she was someone who could both empathise with Adrianna *and* mentor her. Which was so important. There was a long road ahead now – two roads, in fact; one in pursuit of justice and the other to reclaim her child, and it struck me just how important it was that she had a constant, reassuring presence in her life now. Someone she could rely on to support her and guide her through both processes. And I knew that, before long, if all went as planned, that stalwart someone was not going to be me.

I smiled at Jasmine, so young and vibrant, and made a silent heartfelt wish; that nothing changed. That she'd be there to stay the course.

Chapter 16

I loved going to London. In the normal scheme of things, anyway. I loved going to London for all the reasons anyone would. For the musicals. The shopping. The history and culture. For the palaces and parks. The sumptuous hotels. For the sheer exuberant bigness of it all.

On the other hand, more often than not, while I was *on my way* to London, I didn't love going to London at all. First, it was a very long way away, so the drive there seemed interminable. Second, the rail prices were enough to make your hair stand on end, unless you booked six months in advance, when there was a full moon in Neptune and did not, under any circumstances, miss your allocated train, on pain of paying an excess fare that could probably buy a small car. (No wonder Adrianna had always been so wedded to the humble coach.) Third, though the idea of flying there seemed exotic, there was just this thing I had – as with pulling out my mum's posh cups and saucers – that it was something that seemed, well, bizarre.

'And besides,' Mike had pointed out when we'd pondered our options, 'London's so big that by the time we'd found some way from whichever airport to wherever the place we needed to be was, we'd have been better off driving in the first place.'

So, just like every other time we'd gone to London, we drove. Or, rather, we had been driven, and we were currently on the M25 – 'Britain's biggest car park', as hardened commuters apparently put it – on our way to reunite Adrianna with her baby.

Having refrained from scaring Adrianna completely witless during the first part of the meeting, the two police officers had said their farewells and left us. They had taken another copy of Adrianna's birth certificate and some further details about her movements around the UK, and told her they'd be in touch in the next couple of days to pick her up and take her to the Victim Support Unit, where she could make her formal statement.

It would be a process that could, they warned, take several hours, as there was such a lot of ground to be covered. But they reassured her that they'd take her through it every step of the way and that she had nothing to fear in terms of repercussions from any of the gang members. Only after that – and a while after that, in all probability – would they ask her to cast her eye over any 'mug shots'.

'Why do they call them mug shots?' Adrianna had asked me, immediately after they left.

'It's a slang term,' I explained – 'as in "ugly mug" – mug meaning face.'

'Why face?' she'd then wanted to know. To which I said I didn't know the answer. And there followed a conversation about where the term really came from, Jasmine pointing out that the term 'mug' also meant sucker, and John chipping in with 'mugger', which none of us had thought about, all of which diffused the tension very nicely.

And then to the good bit, which was the news John had to impart – that the couple who were currently taking care of the baby were called Jack and Sarah, and that they already had a four-year-old boy of their own. And, best of all, that they were currently just 'testing the water' with fostering, doing short-term placements to see if the fostering lifestyle suited them.

The words 'short-term' were key. It wasn't necessary to say more than that, so John obviously didn't, but we both knew – Jasmine too – that this was good news indeed. Had they been a young, childless couple fostering with a view to adoption it might have been a very different story. This was a common scenario when it came to placing babies, because adoptive parents, like mothers who wished to be reunited with their own children, often went through an initial period of fostering in order to increase their chances of being accepted. It was almost like an item to improve their CVs.

That they weren't in this category could not have mattered more here. Because given that they'd been taking care of him for close on three months now, it would have been just awful for everybody concerned.

So far, so good, then. As was the fact that they were very happy for Adrianna to come and visit just as soon as she liked.

'And do you want to know what his name is?' John asked her.

Adrianna nodded.

'They called him Ethan,' he said, 'after the policeman who found him.'

'Ee-than.' Adrianna tested the word on her tongue. And, for myself, I couldn't help thinking 'awww'. And it also made me wonder about that day, far, far into the future, when Adrianna would have to think hard and make the decision about what, if anything, she should tell him about how he came into the world, and how he came by his first name. Not to mention who his biological father was. Where on earth would you start? Such a difficult decision to have to make.

Such a difficult thing to have to think about, even. Adrianna hadn't brought it up and, taking her lead, neither had I, but it must surely have crossed her mind what kind of man – or rather, monster – his father was. Thank God I believed in the power of nurture over nature, I decided, because if she had asked me, my reassurance that she mustn't even *think* about those genes would at least have the benefit of being genuine.

In the meantime, however, she seemed happy with this news, having, I think, understood and accepted how things had to be. In fact, I'd thought about it subsequently, and I wondered how much it even mattered that he kept it, if she didn't want that to be the case. After all, people changed their names all the time, didn't they? And as a toddler, he would not only get used to it very quickly; in a few years' time he'd have no memory of ever having been called anything else.

But my hunch was that Adrianna would respect both the past and the policeman, and let her little boy's first name stay as it was. And another small nugget of joy, to further leaven the meeting, was that it seemed Jasmine had a nephew called Ethan too. And, better still, a son of her own.

'He's just started nursery school,' she explained, 'which is why I'm back working full time. Or, as I like to put it, twenty-five seven.'

'And you have lots I can learn,' Adrianna enthused. Then proceeded, almost as if they were long-lost sisters, to grill Jasmine mercilessly on every aspect of motherhood, from why she'd called her son Jake (after an actor she particularly liked), to what books she read him, to how many teeth he had. And as I listened, I got the impression that, in Jasmine, here was the phrase 'if you want something done, ask a busy person' personified.

And Jasmine was clearly the poster girl for working motherhood. She hadn't joined us in the car for our trip down this morning because she was already going to be in London on a course, having left Mr Jazz (the kids she'd worked with apparently loved it that she called her partner that, and it had stuck) in charge of Jake overnight. 'Which means he'll have his nappy pants on back to front and his clothes on inside out,' she'd explained to me when we were on the phone making arrangements, 'but I'm sure it'll be character building for them both.'

And with the traffic finally moving I'd just got my phone out to text her, so she knew what time to expect us. 'What's our ETA?' I asked Mike. 'Half an hour?'

'Or thereabouts,' he said.

'So we are nearly there now?' Adrianna asked from the back seat.

Because I was keen that Mike drive us and a weekend was out of the question, almost a fortnight had passed since we'd had our formal meeting, and she'd wished every day of it away. If she'd had a calendar in her room she would probably have taken a pen and marked crosses on it, like a convict. But now the day had come she had become quiet and withdrawn. She'd been unable to stomach breakfast, and, when we stopped midway at the motorway services, had to rush to the loos because she thought she was going to be sick.

I'd bought some travel-sickness pills at the services, hoping they'd help settle her a little, and she subsequently slept the rest of the way.

I twisted around to take a look at her. 'Not far now,' I said. 'How are you feeling, sweetheart? Still nervous?'

'A bit,' she said, rubbing her eyes. 'In fact a big bit,' she corrected. 'No ants in my pants today. But I'm okay, I will be fine.' She wiped a hand across her window and peered out. 'It seems a very long way away.'

We'd almost reached our motorway junction, and I peered ahead too. We were actually on the outskirts of north London, which was a blessing, at least. Had the baby been fostered somewhere central it would have added a lot to the journey.

Mike must have read my thoughts. 'Never ceases to amaze me just how many people seem to be on the move at any time in this place,' he mused. 'It's like a permanent rush hour, isn't it? Where are they all *going*?'

'I read somewhere that building the M25 changed people's habits to a degree they'd never envisaged,' I said. 'That people started taking jobs huge distances away precisely *because* it had been built. Commuting distances they'd never have dreamed of before. It's something to think about, isn't it? That people are prepared to spend such a big chunk of their days just getting from one place to another. I think it would drive me mad. Such a waste of *time*. Speaking of which,' I added, reading the message that had just appeared on the screen of my smartphone, 'Jasmine reckons she's almost there. Says it's taken her almost an hour just from where her course is.'

'She will be there before us, then?' Adrianna asked. 'So she will see my baby before me?'

'I imagine so, sweetheart,' I said, wondering why she'd asked that.

'And me. Will she tell them that I am not a bad person? Do they know about me? I keep thinking. Will they hate me for leaving him?'

'Oh, lord, Adrianna. *No*. No, they won't think that at *all*.

They will have been told all about what happened to you and they will understand why you had to leave him. And, remember, you didn't abandon him. You took him some-where where he would be safe – precisely so people like them could take care of him while you couldn't. I'm sure they are lovely,' I added. 'Just you wait and see.'

Of course, I had no way of knowing that would be the case, because I didn't know them from Adam, but, in this, too, I trusted my instinct. It took a special kind of family to take on the commitment and stress of caring for a new-born baby – it definitely wasn't something for everyone, as anyone who's ever had a newborn baby in their lives will already know. Just like any other parents of newborns they would be chronically sleep deprived, so, even though they had the benefit of confidence – having done it once, with their own son – there was no way around the sheer 24-hour grind of it all.

But as we pulled up outside their neat semi I had a hunch that they were coping just fine. Spring springs early down in London and their square of front garden was already shrugging off its heavy winter blanket, overseen by a flow-ering cherry sitting in the centre of a circular lawn, which made everything look at pretty as a picture.

And the impression was only increased when the front door opened – even as we were clambering stiffly from the car – to reveal a smiling young woman in jeans and a spot-ted sweater. 'Hello!' she said in greeting. 'You made it!'

Adrianna's reaction to her was curious. It was almost as if she shrank a little, as the reality of their disparity sank in.

The disparity that, being an intelligent girl, she couldn't fail to notice, between their ages and situation. And seeing the way she eyed her – with a kind of wariness, tempered, perhaps, by embarrassment – made me think about what an emotional ordeal this must be. She had come to claim her child – her biological child, whom she had a visceral love and need for – and was now faced with the reality that the child was probably happy. And well fed and cared for, and in a better place than he might have been – such a very great deal to take on board.

I gave silent thanks for the knowledge that this couple had no apparent desire to keep him. That like me, they did what they did driven by other motivations; to do their bit. To help in a crisis. To help children, plural. If it worked out that way, anyway. If they decided it was, in fact, for them.

I took Adrianna's hand – something that had become increasingly natural. Though it might slightly diminish her, making her seem very much the gauche, dependent teenager in the woman's eyes, the trade-off was the support that was transmitting now between us. She gripped my hand back and held it tightly as we walked up the path.

Mike brought up the rear, clutching the back of his spine and protesting about his aching back, as you do. Her answering commiserations, and offer of a restorative cup of tea, made for a good and welcome ice-breaker.

As did the appearance of Jasmine, emerging into the hall from a front room as we entered. 'Oh, Adrianna,' she said immediately, grasping her and hugging her. 'He is gorgeous! He is *gorgeous.*' She held her at arm's length again. 'And how are *you?*'

What a difference ten days could make, I thought, as introductions were made and coats were shed. Since the meeting, Jazz had both been round for a more informal visit and made a phone call, seeming to have a natural instinct for making that important early bond with the people in her care.

'Scared and happy all at once,' Adrianna said, with her usual directness.

'Oh, I'll bet,' said the foster mother, Sarah. 'Come on, let's put you out of your misery, shall we?'

We all trooped into a sunny living room – an IKEA room-set kind of living room. All blonde wood and pale rugs and clean, simple lines. And in the midst of it, in contrast, was a splash of poster-paint colour; a baby floor gym – a play mat, complete with hanging mobile.

And in the midst of *that* ... Well, it was difficult to get a proper look initially, as Adrianna, with a sob, seemed to float down to the floor, unhooking her bag from her shoulder, looping her long hair behind her ears, and sinking to her knees before the baby, almost as if in supplication.

We all exchanged looks, like a celebratory gathering would clink glasses, all content just to stay within the moment. And Jazz had been right. He was undeniably gorgeous. Dark haired, like his mother, with berry-bright eyes that gazed up at her with the unquestioning joy of discovery so common in babies of that age, waving his arms and kicking out delightedly with his legs. It was one for the memory banks and I half wished I'd whipped out my phone to capture it – it really was like something out of a photoshoot.

'Oh, my beautiful baby boy,' she sobbed, just staring and staring. Then wiping away tears, lest they spill on him. 'Oh, my little boy.'

The foster dad, Jack, touched both Mike and me on the shoulder, and made the sign for sipping from a cup. 'Was it tea, then, or coffee?'

We both told him the latter and Mike followed him across the hall into the kitchen, there to chat, no doubt, about the state of Britain's road network. I stayed, standing with Jazz, while Sarah approached Adrianna. 'Pick him up, honey. He's your baby,' she said. 'I bet he's missed you.'

Adrianna looked up at her as if she couldn't quite believe what she'd just heard. Then she scooped him up, at first tentatively, but then with an obvious confidence – perhaps as the words had fully sunk in. She groaned softly as she held him to her, cradling his head close to her face. You could almost see the intoxication as she drank the scent of him in.

And in that instant I wished I could wave my own magic wand so that the whole lengthy business of her re-establishing her right to him could be erased – so that she could simply take him home. She was speaking to him now too, whispering streams of words that none of us understood.

Though the content would have been obvious to any mother, in any language, which only increased my sense of frustration.

But the moment was fleeting. Perhaps such a situation would work in fairy tales, but the real world was a very different place. This was a 16-year-old girl, far from family support. And all the love in the world, pure and unconditional as it was, did not make a future for a vulnerable baby. Adrianna had a mountain to climb yet, and she knew it, which was perhaps why she was busy drinking in every drop of this first contact, the culmination of the long, long road trip we'd made this morning, adding our sixpence-worth to the traffic on the M25.

We didn't stay with the family that long. We'd been promised an hour, which was usual, and, as it usually did when a contact meeting was precious to all parties, it went by in a flash. I had a cuddle, as did Mike, and there was the usual baby chit-chat, about how he slept, whether he had colic, what sort of baby he had been. Which made it all very natural, and our chatter created a pleasant background hum, at the centre of which Adrianna cuddled and played with her baby who, to his credit (or his foster mum's), seemed perfectly content to have this young stranger giving him her undivided attention. And I was relieved. It would certainly nourish her till the next time they met, and reminded me how lucky it was that he was still sub-six months, when stranger anxiety and attachment issues usually kicked in. How awful would it have been if she'd come to be reunited with him, only to have him scream his lungs off the moment she picked him up?

Jazz, throughout all this, took a back seat. And literally – choosing a kitchen chair in the corner on which to sit and just observe. For that was as big a part of her job as any other in this process. To observe and report on Adrianna as the baby's mother – her observations, and the recommendations she made subsequent to them, would play a big part in Adrianna having him returned to her.

And it seemed the first hurdle had been negotiated successfully. Hard though it was for Adrianna to leave Ethan, she managed it with composure, buoyed in part by Jasmine confirming, as we prepared to get in our respective cars, that on the basis of this visit she was happy to recommend another. She lingered a while, too, waving alongside the couple as we drove away, and I wondered if she was giving them an impromptu debrief, discussing the practicality – or otherwise – of Ethan being billeted so far away. I hoped so.

But as surely as the joy of it all was lifting Adrianna up now, I knew there would be a long way to fall. And joyous she was – the journey home again could not have been more different. It was as if she'd been slipped a dose of some euphoria-inducing drug. She talked about the baby non-stop all the way to our break at the services, about how Jazz was sorting everything out, about how she couldn't wait to hold her son in her arms again, how she was counting the days, about the things that she'd buy for him and the fun they would have, right down to how she was planning to decorate his room once they finally had their own little home.

'With whitewashed walls, ivy around the front door and a picket fence?' I wondered aloud to Mike, while, a burger and chips dispatched to assuage her sudden appetite, she'd gone off to the loo. 'I see a great fall on the horizon.'

'Course,' Mike said, nodding. 'I think we can take that as read, love … but for the moment, she's fine as she is, rabbiting on. She's bound to be excited and full of plans, isn't she? Even if they are a little pie in the sky yet. Be time to talk some sense to her tomorrow, once she's had a chance to sleep on it.'

And he was right. She'd have that come-down, and it would hit her like a sledgehammer. So, in the meantime, who was I to burst her bubble?

Chapter 17

The fall, when it came, was spectacular. The downward trajectory started the very next day with a call from the police, and the news that, assuming it worked for us, they'd like to collect Adrianna at the beginning of the following week and take her to the Victim Support Unit, and take a full statement from her.

Though if I saw it as a fall, Adrianna was remarkably composed. 'I will be safe there,' she told me. 'I know about such places. A friend of mine had to make a statement about a man who had done some bad things to her. She said it was a good thing. That they were kind. He went to prison.'

'What friend?' I asked, almost automatically, as was my way.

'It's history now, Casey. I don't like to talk about this any more.'

And I didn't push it. It wasn't my job to, and my hunch was that it would be pointless anyway. Adrianna had her own way of processing the past and I had to respect that.

And it seemed she also had her own way of processing the present, because when she was returned to me, four hours after they'd come and collected her, she was again composed and sanguine, even smiling.

'They were so nice,' she said, as I planted a cup of tea between her hands. 'So friendly. And I think I have been helpful. It feels as if I have made my heart lighter, you know?'

I said I did. 'And did they ask you to look at any photographs?'

She shook her head. 'They explained that would come later – another time, when they have made further investigations.'

'So that's good,' I said. 'But you're okay, yes?'

She smiled. 'I feel fine. It's history now. So I don't have to talk about it any more.'

Which I took to be her polite way of once more letting me know that she had no intention of talking about it any more. Which, again, I respected.

But if I had been impressed by the calm way she had coped with the trauma of doing her civic duty, what I hadn't reckoned on was the effect of the news that it looked like Adrianna wouldn't be able to see Ethan again for over a month.

'I'm sorry,' Jazz said, when she called round the following week, 'but I don't honestly see any way around it.'

She'd come to see Adrianna to tell her herself, bless her, and, prudently, we'd timed it so that we'd have a chance to talk before Lauren dropped her off after dance class. That had been one plus, at least – that Adrianna had been very keen to continue helping Lauren out; with no school to attend and the days needing filling, it was at least something to help occupy her time. But this really was a blow, because she was again counting the days.

I couldn't see any way around it either.

'They're going on holiday,' Jazz explained. 'For a fortnight. And it can't be fitted in before they go because I'm up to my eyes on the only days they can do, and that's quite apart from whatever things you and Mike have going on.' She sighed. 'And I know it'll hit her hard but, well, you know how it is.'

I said I did. Because I did. And there was little to be done about it. 'What about him being transferred here?'

Jazz shook her head. 'Not on the cards at this stage, I'm afraid. It's obviously a big upheaval, and he's settled where he is. I know it would make everything so much easier, but it's not like we've got carers for babies queuing round the block – not ones who'd want to commit to something so full-on and open-ended.'

Open-ended was a word that didn't inspire a lot of confidence. But, optimistic as I still was that Adrianna was going to get her baby back eventually, there was no telling how long that would take. It was all too easy to forget that, on top of everything else – not least that she was still an undocumented migrant – she was also a 16-year-old single mother entirely without relatives who could help support her. Which was no small thing for social services to have to take into account.

It was made worse by the fact that Adrianna had bounded in so joyfully, having seen Jazz's car in the road when Lauren dropped her off. She was also full of the fact that Lauren had had to take my youngest grandaughter along to the class, her mum being full of cold, and had put Adrianna in charge of keeping her entertained.

'She is so lovely,' she enthused to Jazz. 'Dee Dee calls me Addy. She's so funny …' And then, presumably seeing the expression on both our faces, she frowned. 'Something has happened,' she said. 'What? Are the police going to make me do the mug shots?'

Jazz was quick to reassure her. 'Nothing like that,' she said. 'It's just your next visit to see Ethan. I'm afraid you are going to have to exercise a little patience.'

'What?' Adrianna said, all her *joie de vivre* forgotten.

'It's going to be a little while, that's all. About a month.'

'A month?' Adrianna said, tears pooling in her eyes, reminding me just how close to the surface they always were currently. I had more than once had to go to her and console her in the night. And she hadn't just been crying about missing Ethan either. It was as if a seed of deep sadness had been growing inside her – perhaps the knowledge that she might be able to form her own family had begun to worm away at the protective shell she'd built around her nightmare, reminding her of the family she used to have. I'd considered more than once asking John if we might try to investigate her wider family – or at least try to facilitate it by getting her a counsellor with whom she could explore the possibility of doing so. But I'd stopped short. She had quite enough to deal with already, what with the police involvement hanging over her, the ramifications of all that and the ever-present anxiety about the outcome with Ethan.

'It can't be helped, sweetheart,' I said. 'All these things need to be organised. And they're going away –'

She looked stricken. 'They can't take my baby away!'

'Not *away* away,' I reassured her. 'Just away for a holiday.'

'But how can they, when they know I need to see him so *much*?'

The phrase 'they have their own child to think about' would have been highly inappropriate, so I parked it. 'A holiday they had *booked*,' I said. 'A long time ago. Before they had Ethan. And it's not so long – the time will pass –'

'But for my baby it is a huge time! He will forget me, and next time I see him he will not *know* me!'

'Yes, he will,' Jazz tried to soothe.

'But he won't! I know he won't. I have read about it. He will become more and more attached to his foster mummy. I know. And it will make it all so much *harder*!'

Jazz caught my eye. Adrianna had indeed been reading books. She'd taken the baby-care book from my bookcase and devoured it, even though it wasn't in her native language. She couldn't have been more motivated to learn the words.

'Sweetheart,' I said gently, 'there is nothing we can do here. Except reassure you that everything that can be done is being done. You have to be *patient*.' I had a thought. 'Tell you what. How about we go into town tomorrow and you can choose something for Ethan – a special present that he can take away with him? And you can write him a note, which Sarah can read to him, and …'

'What is the *point*?' she said, sobbing. 'He is too young to know!'

She fled the kitchen just as Tyler, down from his bedroom, was walking into it, and, for a moment, they were engaged in an almost comic dance as they both tried to dodge each other but ended up going the same way. 'Whoah,' he said, finally coming in as she thundered upstairs. 'What's happened?' He looked at us both in turn. 'What have I missed?'

Once Jazz had gone, having promised to see if there was anything she could do to hurry things along, I started preparing tea, and gave Tyler the gist. 'She needs to get out more, she does,' was his considered opinion once I'd finished. 'You know, get out as in go out a bit. She's got no one her own age to chill with. Well, apart from me,' he added, almost as if challenging me to comment that, actually, he wasn't quite her age yet.

As if I would. She might have been through a lot more than most girls her age, but he'd also been through a great deal. And, as a consequence, though he bore the scars – some of which might not have even began to itch yet – he also had wisdom beyond his years and a kindness about him that rarely failed to move me. I'd never urged him to include Adrianna in his social life, obviously, because that wouldn't have been fair. And once the real picture emerged – both about her age and his crush – I wouldn't have dreamt of doing so. 'You know what?' I said, touched. 'You're absolutely right. She needs to distract herself, doesn't she? You're a sweetheart, you know that?' I made a move to give him a squeeze, to which he grudgingly submitted. 'I'm sure it will help her feel better.'

And beyond the usual concerns any parent would have about youngsters going out, it never occurred to me that it might make things *worse*.

Though she'd only been with us a relatively short time, it still seemed strange, when I thought about it, that she and Tyler had never been out together up to now – not without the family, at least. Not on their own. I said so to Mike late that night, once we'd got into bed and I'd mentioned Tyler's idea that they do so.

He disagreed. 'Not so strange,' he said. 'Not when you think about it. She was ill at first, obviously, then everything blew up, and since then I think the age difference has made for a bit of distance. And it does make a difference; she's almost 17. And a mum. *And* a girl. And he's a 14-year-old boy. Which is not to say it's not a good idea he's had, bless him. But I remember being his age – a 17-year-old girl was like an alien from another planet!'

'They're not going on a *date*,' I reminded him. 'He'd be mortified to think she thought that. She's just going along with him and Denver. And Sam, I think, too …'

'Blimey, her own adoring retinue, then.'

The truth of his words wasn't lost on me. And a part of me thought that perhaps that wasn't a bad thing. The fact that they were younger probably made them feel safe. In any event, when she came down, contrite and apologetic, and he'd suggested it to her, she agreed to the idea readily enough. It was only for a 'mooch about', after all. What could possibly go wrong?

I also thought it all rather sweet. 'What's a mooch about?' she'd asked Tyler, it being a word she'd obviously not come across.

He'd grinned. 'Just, like, mooching. You know, just hanging about,' he said.

'I sincerely hope not,' I countered. 'I hope you'll find something more productive to do that that.'

'Mum, you *know*,' he said. 'It's like we don't have a particular *plan*. We might see a film. Might just go for an ice-cream – we have the wickedest ice-cream parlour down the town centre. Bar *none*. Or we might go bowling.' He shrugged his shoulders. 'We'll just see when we get to it. Keep it loose.'

I had to bite my lip to keep myself from grinning.

In any event, it seemed to go some way in lifting Adrianna's spirits, even to the extent of her asking me, on Friday afternoon before Tyler got home from school, what sort of thing she should wear to go mooching. We ended up settling on her skinny jeans, her black roll-neck jumper and her trainers. God only knew how many miles she'd be expected to trudge, after all. And after feeding them tea and giving them the usual nine-thirty home time, Mike and I waved them off with no more thought in our heads than the reflection that, for this not quite yet 17-year-old girl, this was a long-overdue return to innocence.

By nine thirty I was already fretting. Not because they were late yet, but because quarter of an hour earlier I had called Tyler and got no response. This was unlike him, not least because we'd put a lot of man hours into the business of making it clear that the one thing he must always, always do was respond if we texted or called him. All the freedoms he enjoyed, which were growing along with him, were dependent on this one element of trust. Adhere to that one golden rule – this had always been our mantra – and you will have far fewer other rules as a consequence.

And so far, in the main, it had worked. There'd been the one time when he'd been in the cinema and turned the sound on his mobile off, and, once corroborated, there was no more to be said. And the odd occasion when his battery had died. We weren't naïve, there would be other times down the line – he wasn't an angel. But we'd long ago learned that it was a rule worth enforcing, having seen and heard of too many fraught situations when children, hidebound by a plethora of rules and curfews, responded to the prospect of being commanded home and/or screamed at by simply ignoring their parents, and, as a consequence, potentially putting themselves in danger.

'Perhaps he's just having far too good a time,' Mike chuckled, as I stood peering out through the curtains. He was, as yet, completely unconcerned.

'And it's not like he's on his own,' I conceded, letting the curtain fall again. 'I'm sure they're fine. I'm still going to have a word with him, though, if they're not in by quarter to.'

'Try his mobile again,' he suggested. 'Maybe he had it on vibrate. But, honestly, love, I'm quite sure you're worrying about nothing. He's –'

He didn't finish, because my mobile began dancing on the coffee table. 'There you go,' he said, reaching for it. 'Ah, maybe not.'

I was close enough to see the word 'unknown' on the display, and experienced that pit-of-the-stomach lurch every parent is familiar with, when a child is late home and a call comes.

Mike handed it to me and I swiped the screen to accept the call.

'Casey Watson?' It was a male voice. 'This is PC Anderson from the town centre station. Now it's nothing to be alarmed about,' he added quickly. He was obviously used to making such calls. 'But we have three youngsters down here who have been in a bit of an altercation.'

'*What?*' I spluttered.

'A Tyler, a Denver and – he paused – an Adrianna.' Which he pronounced 'Adri*arrrna*'. 'They belong to you?'

'Mostly,' I said, my mind whirring as I explained who was who, knowing full well that Denver would be only too happy if we claimed him in this particular scenario as our own, having only just been released from a grounding. 'But what's happened?' I pressed, as various scenarios suggested themselves. It was all so unbelievable. What could they have done?

'Probably easiest if you just came down to the station,' the constable said amiably. 'We can explain it all to you while we finish taking their statements. But like I said, it's nothing *too* bad, so don't be worrying.'

'Don't you be worrying?' I said to the phone once I'd checked I'd disconnected. 'Don't you be worrying? In my shoes? Fat chance!'

'Go on, then,' said Mike, taking his cue from my huffing and as a consequence *not* worrying one bit. 'What've they done?'

I told the officer we'd be there in ten minutes, and Mike what little I knew as we sped the couple of miles to the central police station.

'Honestly, I'll bloody kill Tyler if he's done something stupid just to show off to Adrianna,' I fumed to Mike as we pulled up and parked as near as we could. 'I bet that's what's happened. He'll have been over-excited … showing her off to his mates. God, *boys*!'

'Hold your horses, love,' Mike responded – in his usual calm (not to mention irritating) fashion. 'A) You don't know that, and B) *boys*? That's a bit sexist, isn't it? What about girls? We've known a fair few that have led us a merry dance, our own darling daughter included. And hang on. There was this girl I once met … known for dancing on the tables …'

I thumped him before I got out of the car.

He was right, though. I shouldn't make assumptions and go in there with all guns blazing, even if I knew there was a strong possibility Tyler *would* have been over-excited. Despite all Mike's joking about it, there was a truth in what I'd said. 'Mooching' with your mates with a stunning 16-year-old on your arm? He'd have been odd it he hadn't been showing off a bit, wouldn't he?

The officer on the desk, who was the one who had made the call to us, had the air of a man for whom this small, teenage fracas was just the opening scene in his usual Friday-night theatre. Which was to say he was cheerful that it was only a small altercation, as he put it, but resigned that his night could only get worse.

'Follow me,' he said, coming out from behind the counter and directing us. 'I'll take you to the interview room – my colleague is in there with the kids.'

'Are any of them being charged with anything?' Mike asked. 'Have they done something illegal?'

'Oh, I don't think so,' said the constable. 'Nothing to worry about. Just a minor fracas. Here we are. My colleague will put you in the picture.'

We filed in. It was fair to say that it was the kids' faces that were the picture. They were sitting in a row on the far side of a grey, formica-topped table that had some kind of recording equipment on top of it. On the near side was another uniformed officer.

The room was brightly lit, cramped and smelt mildly of disinfectant; just the sort of environment where hardened criminals were apt to crack.

Casey Watson

The constable who'd shown us in took a seat in the corner, and the other one – the one charged with getting to the facts, presumably – swivelled in his seat and nodded a curt hello. I understood his dourness; I'd spent plenty of time with policemen and errant teenagers, and I knew the score. That they had to look fierce and, to that end, invariably stayed in character. I instantly felt reassured, however, that there was nothing terribly serious going down here.

I looked first at Tyler. His face begged to differ. And I realised it was a long time since he'd been in such a situation, and that the memory of previous times was filling his head. It was in this very police station that we had first met, and it wasn't lost on either of us, I don't think.

I certainly wouldn't ever forget it. The first time I clapped eyes on that furious, sullen, tearful (though he hid that pretty well) pubescent, with all his attitude and language and sense of righteous unrepentance – and knew I was going to fight his corner with him. That our lives – Mike's as well – would go on to be bound so inextricably I then *didn't* know. But it wasn't very long before I did.

Taking their lead, I adopted the same expression as the officers. 'Can somebody please tell us what's been going on?' I barked. It wasn't hard to, looking at the trio. As always, when I felt let down by unnecessary shenanigans, I could very easily lose my temper.

'I can do that,' the officer at the table said, angling his chair, the better to speak to us. 'We had a call earlier this evening to attend an incident at The Falls leisure complex. You know it?'

'What?' I said, glaring at Tyler. 'What on *earth* were you doing all the way over there?'

The Falls was a huge complex on the far side of town, housing a cinema, a bowling arcade and various fast-food restaurants. It was also, of course, prime mooching territory for teens. But it was also the last place I'd expect them to go. Too expensive and too far from their 'territory' – especially as there was a perfectly good, albeit smaller, complex on our *own* side of town. Showing off, I thought again. So I'd been right, then.

'Yes,' I said pointedly. 'I *do* know it.'

'Good,' said the officer, as if I'd got a test question right. 'Well, as I say, the call came from a member of the public about a fight that had broken out. Nothing major,' he added while Tyler hung his head, but as it involved several youths' – he looked at Adrianna – 'including a female, and had been going on for a while, we, of course, had to respond, *particularly* as it was taking place in a family restaurant, with families and children witnessing it.'

All three kids looked steadfastly at the floor as he went on to explain the fuller story he'd now established. And it seemed the fight – which had mostly involved Tyler and another boy – had broken out seemingly randomly but, actually, as it turned out, as a result of Tyler intervening in a scrap between the other boy and Adrianna.

I looked at her, genuinely shocked. So *she'd* been fighting? It crossed my mind that I must never forget where she'd come from. From captivity, from the streets, from a life of fear and necessary self-defence.

'The other lad is known to us,' the officer went on. 'The lad scrapping with Adrianna here. We'd gone down originally assuming he was scrapping with your lad, Tyler here, but it seems it wasn't quite so cut and dried. Tyler's just been explaining it all,' he said. 'Why don't you fill your mam in, eh, lad?'

'He was saying all kinds of sh – erm, stuff to her, Mum. Taking the mickey with his mate. Impersonating Adrianna's accent. Like, *really* trying to provoke us. Calling her an immigrant and a slag and that. And I tried to stay calm, honest. But I just couldn't, because he just kept going on. And then she turned round and told them to stop it, and he was, like, "Oh, it speaks *English!*" and really taking the piss. And he was a big lad and he was, like, getting really, *really* lairy with her. And when she shouted back – 'cos she's got to defend herself, hasn't she? – he came round to our table and just spat in her chips. Like, proper spat in them. It was *gross.*' He spread his hands. 'And I just couldn't stop myself, honest. He was asking for it, he really was. So Denver and I got up, and I pushed him, and told him to move it, and then he punched me in the face.'

Only belatedly did I notice the red mark on his far cheek. He was so red generally, from indignation – as were they all – I'd not seen it.

'He is telling you the truth, Casey and Mike,' Adrianna said, clutching at Tyler's hand and squeezing it. 'The man was a disgusting pig. And so big, too. Twice the size of Tyler and Denver. And he really hurt him. I heard the smack on his cheek, and I could do nothing. He was a pig!'

So Adrianna had given him a right hook as well, had she? *Go her*, then, I couldn't help think, albeit privately, just in my own head.

'He didn't hurt me that bad,' Tyler added quickly. This would of course be a question of pride. He then glanced at Adrianna, and I could see him trying hard to suppress a smile. 'But I'm pretty sure Adrianna hurt *him*.'

Mike and I both looked at her. 'I slapped him,' she said defiantly. 'Which he *deserved*. Then the policemen came …'

'… and broke it up,' added Denver, with an unmistakably wistful air.

'I'm sorry, Mum,' Tyler said. 'I know how you feel about this stuff. Please don't be angry. Like Adrianna said, he got exactly what he deserved.'

Actually, I *was* furious, but not at any of these three. No, it was at what I had just heard – which had repulsed me. There was a part of me that wanted to march straight to wherever the other lad was being interviewed – which I presumed must be the case – and give him a piece of my mind. There was something so abhorrent about what he'd done, and I wanted to make him see that. Because spitting, to me, was such a foul, aggressive act. It made such a powerful, unambiguous point about the way a person felt about another person. Exhibited so clearly the disgust in a person's mind. And in this case, it was evidence of the worst kind of racism. Knee-jerk. Uncompromising. Taking no account of the human being before you. Treating a fellow human as *sub*-human.

So, yes, a huge part of me felt proud of Tyler and Denver coming to Adrianna's defence. It showed their true colours. That they were *not* like that. And though I'd never condone them starting a fight, I could understand how angry they must have felt.

I turned to the officer again. 'But you're not bringing any charges? Is that still the case?'

He shook his head, 'No. Under the circumstances, we're satisfied that this little bunch are the ones who were being attacked. The other lad is already known to us for this sort of thing, Mrs Watson.' He turned to the kids. 'So as we're about done, you're all free to go.'

But he wasn't quite done. There was always room for a little light reinforcement of the laws of the land. He narrowed his eyes and looked hard at the three of them once again. 'Though you might want to reiterate to Tyler what we've already told him, Mr and Mrs Watson – about racist attacks and the best thing to do. Which is *not* to retaliate, however powerful the provocation, but to step away and telephone *us*. It's a serious offence is this kind of racism, and scrapping's not the answer. If we're to clamp down on it properly it needs dealing with equally seriously. By the authorities. Not by fisticuffs. Clear?'

'Oh, we'll definitely be doing that,' Mike assured the officer. And as he did so, I thought about the old ladies in my sister's restaurant and how their own brand of idle, everyday, throwaway racism was what contributed to the attitudes of boys such as the one our three had unfortunately encountered tonight. Those old ladies who'd been so cruel to Adrianna probably all had families; kids and grandkids, nieces and nephews, who would also have friends, and the whole lot of them could come within the circle of ignorance. And the worst of it was that it was so insidious; their ill-informed gossip, about what they thought immigrants and foreigners were doing to *their* country, was probably transmitted to the next generation without anyone ever noticing – not thinking about it, or debating it, or discussing the facts, and so it went on. It was all just so depressing.

'Well, Rocky Balboa,' Mike said to Tyler as soon as we were back in the car. 'That was your version of mooching then, was it? And what the hell were you doing all the way down at The Falls when we've got a perfectly good place to go round our way?'

Denver, who we were dropping home, was shuffling uncomfortably in the back seat. 'Actually, Mike,' he said quietly, 'that was my fault. I'd gone to my gran's for tea and couldn't be bothered walking all the way back.' Which made sense, I conceded, because his gran did live over that way. 'I asked Ty and Adrianna to come meet me – my gran had given me a bit of money, like – so I said I'd buy the chips if they did.'

'Well, you're lucky you didn't all get porridge for your breakfast too, by the sound of it!' Mike said as he drove up Denver's street. I could tell he felt pleased with himself, and we both had to hide our smiles, but when I turned around, all three of them looked at me blankly. I didn't bother to elaborate.

'Well, all's well that ends well,' I said, as Mike pulled up to let Denver out. 'Let's officially put this evening to one side and move on, eh?' I glanced at Mike, and he nodded, then nodded at Denver. 'As far as we're concerned, this is the end of the matter,' he said to him pointedly, meaning that there seemed no need for us to give his mum chapter and verse.

He smiled gratefully at us as he waved, then scooted into his house, and we headed home relieved that it had not been any worse. That we could put it to one side and forget all about it.

Or so I thought. But before the next 24 hours were out, we would be learning a very harsh lesson.

Chapter 18

By the Wednesday of the following week the incident had been relegated to its proper place in everyone's lives; i.e. I had forgotten all about it, Adrianna wanted to forget all about it and Tyler wanted to milk it for all it was worth. Some things with teenage boys are almost universal.

And Adrianna really did want to forget all about it, and when she heard him bragging about it on his mobile, as he was coming in from school – and for the umpteenth time, too – she finally confronted him.

'Tyler, I *wish* you wouldn't do that,' she said after he'd finished on the phone. 'Telling everyone what happened. It makes me feel stupid.'

Tyler grinned and threw his jacket onto one of the coat pegs in the hall. 'Don't be daft,' he said. 'Why should *you* feel stupid? You did nothing wrong, it was that meathead that had a go at us, so he's the one who'll be feeling stupid.' Or more likely aggrieved, I imagined, the constable having called us subsequently to say he had, in fact, been formally cautioned.

Tyler puffed himself up as he tugged down the waist-band of his school hoodie. 'And I'd do it again if I had to,' he said proudly. 'No one has the right to treat you like that.'

Seeing the way Adrianna looked at him, I decided to step in. 'Tyler, less of that fighting talk, love, okay? Didn't I say the other day that we should just all forget it?'

He looked like he was about to interrupt, so I held up my hand. 'Enough. Let's let it go now shall we?. I know you're proud of having stood up for her, but Adrianna would just like to forget it now. Dad'll be home any minute, so go on, go up and sort out your laundry, so I can get a wash on and crack on with your tea before the pizza's burned.'

Since Tyler had strong opinions about the done-ness of his pizzas, it was enough to send him scooting, with a grin, up the stairs.

'Don't worry,' I told Adrianna as she helped me dish out side salads. 'Boys are like that. It makes them feel macho.'

'Macho?' she asked, confused. Not a word she was famil-iar with, obviously. I put down the pizza wheel and flexed my muscles, Popeye-style.

She grinned. 'Big muscles, then?'

'Big attitude.'

'That's funny,' she said. 'Tyler told me they were called bingo wings.'

'Oh, did he now?' I said. 'Cheeky little tyke. For that I think I might just turn the oven up a notch while the pizza finishes off!'

I couldn't help but smile, though. It was always the little things that got me, every time. I loved that Tyler teased me – felt secure enough to do so. He was no different now, in many ways, to how Kieron was at his age. And that spoke volumes, because Kieron had had such a different start in life. A childhood in which he was enveloped in love and a sense of security – not only our love, but the warm, enveloping blanket of his wider family, too. Tyler had been denied that, so cruelly, so any hint that he felt secure meant the world to me.

He'd come such a long way since coming to live with us – testament to the support of so many people, both in the family, and outside it, too – the support of John, his wonderful social worker, Will, the whole machinery of social services that really did have the power to transform lives, even if sometimes the tabloids did tear them to pieces.

I thought about Adrianna too, already 16 and having been through so much, and wondered if she was now too old to be given the same opportunities to similarly flourish. I really hoped she wasn't. In an ideal world, social services would plan to get on board 100 per cent with her, facilitate as much contact with her baby as possible, move him closer to us in order to *make* all this possible. And then, finally, get her somewhere safe to live, and set about giving her baby back to her full time. I couldn't have wished for that more.

But I was also a realist. Happy endings were few and far between in the world of fostering, and I knew as much as anyone that we didn't live in an ideal world. Though, for all that, the one thing I *wasn't* expecting was to have that spelled out to me quite so quickly.

We'd only just finished tea when my mobile rang. I was in the kitchen cleaning the pots and pans while everyone else was playing cards. Adrianna was rather good at cards, and had taught Mike and Tyler a couple of new games – one of the more positive aspects of her time living as a squatter, it turned out, where entertainment, when not of the chemical variety, was usually of the extremely cheap sort.

Seeing John's name come up on the display, I quickly dried my hands and reached for it.

'Sorry to bother you,' he said, 'but do you have a few minutes to talk in private?'

The doors into the dining area of the living room were half closed. I knew I was probably safe enough in the kitchen. I pushed the door closed. 'What?' I said, anxious to know what it was we had to talk about in private, and feeling the familiar heart sink that it probably wasn't great news. Another delay in the next contact visit, perhaps?

No. It was worse. Far, far worse. 'It's about the incident over at The Falls,' he said.

'Really?' My heart sank even further. So what could have happened? I racked my brain, riffling through possibilities. Might the boy in question's parents have made some sort of counter-claim? It seemed unlikely that they'd do that, especially if he already had previous. On what grounds? 'What about it?' I said.

John sighed. 'Well, like you, I'd obviously put the whole episode to bed. Filed your report. Signed it off – such as it was, which seemed to be nothing. Job done. But I'm afraid the gods seem to have other plans for us.'

I was confused. 'I don't understand, John. What gods? What's happened?'

'There's been a complaint.'

So was I right about the boy? Or someone else? 'A complaint?' I said. 'What, by someone who was there and witnessed it? What kind of complaint?'

'Someone who witnessed it, yes –'

'But the police said it was something and nothing. That they were satisfied Tyler did nothing wrong. He was the one *hit*, for goodness' sake. God, I wish I'd taken a photo of the bloody bruise now, so we could show it to them. John, I know he didn't start anything. I know he's not an angel, but ...'

'Casey,' John said, almost sharply. 'The complaint wasn't about Tyler. It was about Adrianna.'

'*What?*' Now I was truly stunned. 'What?' I said again. 'What on earth for? What could anyone possibly complain about with *her*?'

'Not a lot, as far as I'm concerned, which is why I was as flabbergasted as you were. But then it struck me – the complaint was sent directly to my boss.'

'Your boss? How would some random person ...' Now my mind was reeling. 'What did they say about her anyway?'

'Oh, that she was fighting and swearing and lots of other stuff like that. Most tellingly, that she wasn't fit to be a *mother*.'

He emphasised that last word. 'Go on,' I said. 'What's the punchline to all this?

'Casey, it was that Mr Kanski. Remember? The interpreter who came round with me when Adrianna was first with you.'

'Good God,' I said, truly stunned now. '*Really?*'

'Really. As soon as I read it, I thought, "Hang on, what can this person possibly know about all of this stuff?" How would they even know she was in care, for one thing? So I turned it over to check who'd written it, expecting it to be anonymous – you know, signed by a "concerned party", that sort of thing. But not at all. No cloak and dagger stuff. No, he was obviously happy to put his name to it. He even added the bloody letters after it, too.'

What, his degree in inexplicable spite? I was fuming. 'I don't bloody believe this,' I said, feeling the tendrils of gloom curling round me. I couldn't make sense of it, I really couldn't. I just felt really, really cross.

'So he was there at the McDonald's or wherever it was?'

'Apparently so.'

'Bloody hell, what an unfortunate flipping co-incidence.'

'Not really. It was a Friday evening. He lives over that way. It's the place loads of families fetch up to start their weekends, isn't it? Might have just come out of the pictures, or something ...'

'So if that's so, and he recognised her, why the hell didn't he step in and do something about it? Call the manager? Stop the lad terrorising her? Do the decent thing and help her *out*?'

Because that made no sense either. That he'd just stand by and let something like that happen. Even taking into account the fact that he was so grumpy and taciturn, he was an older man, and one who knew the straits Adrianna had been in before she'd come to us. And added to that was the fact that the lad had been hurling racial taunts at her, and Mr Kanski was Polish *himself*! Of all the people you'd think would come to her aid at such a time ... It made no sense at *all*. I was flummoxed.

I said as much to John. 'I know,' he said, 'both the boss and I are as well. But that's what he's done – and copied it to social services by all accounts. A very long and damning letter about her brawling and shouting and appearing to have no morals. I'll show it to you when I see you. It's poisonous, it really is. And it ends with the damaging recommendation, as I say, that in his professional opinion she isn't fit to be a mother.'

'But how does he even *know* about that? *We* didn't even know – not till long after he'd been to the house!'

'He does a fair bit of work for the council. Obviously has some friends in various sufficiently high places.'

'But why would he victimise her like that?'

'Beats me,' John said. 'Unless there's something we don't know, that is.'

'But what?'

'I don't *know*. But there's something else too. He reckons in his letter that she was under the influence of alcohol.'

'What! Well that's baloney. No way is that true. We were with them half an hour later and they were all stone cold sober. I'd stake my life on it. And I'm not being naïve here. I would *know*, John. Jeez, I've dealt with enough inebriated teenagers in my time. That's an out-and-out lie.'

'And it reads like one. But you know what I'm going to say, don't you? There's a process that is going to need to happen now ...'

'But John,' I interrupted, still fired up by my train of thought. 'The police attended. They have all the statements. They were witnesses themselves. They can confirm this is all patent nonsense. Has anyone spoken to them?'

'I spoke to them myself earlier, and they've agreed to get something put in writing and sent to me. But you know how it goes, Casey. This will all take time. You can't just have access to confidential police statements at the drop of a hat.'

I knew that all too well. The wheels of justice turned ridiculously slowly. 'And until then?'

'Until then, no further contact with the baby. I'm so sorry. I hate to be saying this, but I just don't have any wriggle room here.'

I think I actually groaned. 'But that's so un*fair*. How can the lies of one vindictive old man cause such chaos? It'll go on her record too, won't it?'

'Only as a note. And with another one, God willing, to confirm that it's unsubstantiated.'

'Yeah, much good that'll do. You know as well as I do how these things work. No smoke, and all that. God, John, this is *terrible.*'

I felt impotent; was absolutely apoplectic with anger.

'I know, Casey,' John said, 'but what can I do? Well, bar hurry the police up, which I shall try to. I'll do my absolute best, I promise, because I'm as flabbergasted as you are. What can he possibly have against her? I can't imagine. Can you? Was there anything you can think of about that visit that might have triggered this? Because I can't. And no follow-up?'

'You know there wasn't.'

'Did he call at all?'

'No, of *course* not. It's not like I'd have forgotten to tell you if he had, is it? Because it would have just been so weird. And why on earth would he have something against a fellow Pole?'

'I have no idea,' John said. 'Perhaps we're reading too much into it. Perhaps he's just one of those types who has a downer on young people generally. Perhaps it's nothing to do with their nationality. Perhaps it's just plain spite. Or perhaps he really does believe everything he says. Perhaps he's saving the world from the youths of today one youth at a time. I suppose in his line of work he spends a lot of time with society's misfits and wasters …'

'Neither of which she is. Grrr, I could *so* swear myself now. God, and what do I tell her? The poor girl is on pins enough as it is, and she's so looking forward to seeing the baby again.'

John sighed. 'I just don't know what to tell you, Casey,' he said, 'but my instinct is to tell her nothing. Unless you have reason to believe she knows it's part of some personal vendetta, I'd say nothing. Just talk about logistics taking time and so on, while I try to sort it all out. Which I will do, I promise.'

John was right, I thought, as I ended the call and put my phone back on the counter. I definitely couldn't say anything to Adrianna – not until I knew for sure what might happen. And as for the no-contact thing, she didn't need to know about that either. I would just have to brush any awkward questions to one side and try to find things to keep her busy.

And in the way that things sometimes come to you, I had a brainwave only seconds later. Mike and the kids were still playing cards, the laughter bubbling across the hall to me in snatches. Which would normally be a delightful thing to hear. But knowing what I knew just made the sound of it depress me. What was *wrong* with the bloody world!

I took a deep, slow breath. Nothing was going to come of this. It was just an irritating hiccup. One I could manage. *We* could manage, as a family. I swiped the lock screen on my mobile and scrolled through my contacts. I would make a call to my sister, and then a further one to Lauren.

An observer might deduce that I was powered by some sort of hyperdrive, fuelled by anger and a sense of injustice. And they'd have been absolutely right. And it was productive, too, because no more than 20 minutes later I had some extremely good news to impart. That, starting that very weekend, Adrianna would be the new part-time waitress at Truly Scrumptious, filling the slot that my niece Chloe had temporarily relinquished, so she could begin revising in earnest for her A levels. And also that Adrianna's help at Lauren's dance classes would henceforth be on a more formalised footing. She'd now help out twice a week, utilising her impressive dance credentials.

No, it wouldn't help a jot in the matter of the inexplicable Mr Kanski. But it made me feel better – in a yin and yang, cosmic-balancing sort of way (at least *some* of us were actually *helping* our young people, I raged) – and it would also keep Adrianna busy enough, hopefully, that the delay in seeing Ethan wouldn't be quite so hard to bear.

And she was predictably delighted. 'Oh, I will be such a busy bee!' she said. 'Or is it wasp?'

I rolled my eyes at Tyler, who sniggered. 'It's definitely bee, love.'

'And I can save money. Lots of money. So I can buy things for Ethan.'

'And I'll tell you what we'll do,' I said. 'We'll go into town next week and get a savings account opened for you.'

'Without a passport?'

'No, that's fine. I'm sure your birth certificate will be enough. That way you can start getting into a regular habit, can't you?'

'And be a properly independent Polish girl!' she said, laughing. 'Not one of those scroungers off the plate!'

I wasn't sure exactly where she'd got that gem, but I laughed along with her. Though not inside. Inside I was *seething*.

Chapter 19

'I'm not sure that's your decision to make,' Mike said, shaking his head.

It was almost midnight, and though I'd gone through the motions of a jolly family evening, there was a part of me that was itching to get to bed so I could fill Mike in on the conversation I'd had with John. And he'd been unsurprised when I launched into a torrent of angry yammering the minute we closed our bedroom door.

'I knew there was something,' he'd said, grinning. 'I knew you were a bit manic. All that busy-bee stuff and organising Adrianna's life to the nth degree.'

Neither of us was grinning now.

'Seriously,' he said, 'I don't agree with John on this one. I mean, I know you absolutely believe what the kids have told you about what happened – and I do too. But what if there is more to this? There is still so much we don't know about Adrianna, isn't there? Supposing she has had some interaction with this man?'

Mike hadn't met him so it was obviously hard for him to judge what sort of man he was. 'But when would she? How? Bar a couple of trips to the shop for me, she's barely been out of our sight since she came to us! Mine or Lauren's, at any rate. How can there be any more to this? I don't see it.'

Pyjamas on, Mike clambered into bed. 'Love, come on – think. What about the internet? Facebook? Insta-whatever? Twitter? How do you know she's not been on the web and got herself involved with the local Polish commu-nity?' He looked at my expression. 'I'm not talking about anything dodgy here, for goodness' sake. I'm just talking about making friends. Chatting to other young people who speak her language.'

I hadn't thought of that. Why hadn't I thought of that? 'God, and you think he might be part of the same community and be, like, stalking her?' It was too grim a thought to contemplate. I refused to contemplate it. But though I didn't think for a moment that he would have anything to do with the monsters who'd trafficked her – they were hopefully halfway across the country – she was an attractive young girl, and ... 'God, Mike. I can't believe that.'

'I'm not suggesting you "believe" anything. I just think you should consider sitting her down and asking her if she can think of any reason that this man could have it in for her. Don't forget, she's been keeping a lot of secrets over a long time. If she has had any dealings with him –'

'I just don't believe it's possible.'

'But if she has … Love, I'm just saying that she's used to playing her cards close to her chest, that's all. And we should give her the opportunity to open up.'

'I suppose …' I said, still feeling angsty about that course of action.

'And another thing before this light goes off and we go to sleep – I have to be up at six, remember – you don't know all the story. All you've had corroborated by the police is what happened after they got there. Now, as I say, I trust Tyler, and I'm certain we have the full picture, but if there's been an allegation of drinking then I think you should at least *ask* them about it. Who's to say they didn't get some alcohol from somewhere – now, just *stop* that,' he said, seeing my bulging eyeballs. 'It's been *known*. Earlier on, say. And given what's happened, we need to give them a chance to tell us anything they haven't as yet. So we are armed and able to fight any allegations that might be made.'

'Have been made.'

'Might be made. By panel. If they decide to take this nonsense seriously. Okay?'

'Okay,' I said. Because Mike was right. What did I know? Whatever we thought of the man, he was a professional in some capacity, and he'd put a complaint in against a child who was in care. And they *might* take it seriously.

I lay there and ruminated on it for a good 15 minutes, agonising over the thing I knew I had to do. I didn't believe for a minute that this was anything but a bunch of trumped-up nonsense – for whatever reason – and I felt wretched at the thought that, because of it, I was potentially going to have to shatter the trust that had begun to grow between us and Adrianna – and, more importantly, between Adrianna and the society in which she'd begun to place that trust.

Then I turned to Mike. 'Are you still awake?' I asked him. He grunted an affirmative. 'I'm still not sure,' I whispered. 'I just wonder if we shouldn't leave it for a bit and see what happens first.' Then I burbled on about my thinking on trust.

He turned to face me. 'Yes. You are right about the trust, Case. But that's *exactly* why you need to explain things as they really are. She needs to know that we are being honest with her, that she *can* trust us and that we *will* fight for her. Look, she's already had knocks and has proved she can deal with them, hasn't she? And this time she won't be on her own, will she? She'll have us in her corner. And that will *build* trust.'

I perhaps should have trusted my own instinct. Opting to say nothing to Tyler till I knew where we were at with Adrianna (there was no *way* I was going to accuse him of not telling us the truth, because I refused to believe, given everything that had flowed under the bridge, that he'd even *consider* abusing the trust we had placed in him), I waited till he'd left for school the following morning before sitting down and telling Adrianna about our new 'development'.

It took a while, because I was keen to make Mike's and my position clear; filling her in about the feelings I'd had about Mr Kanski back in January, and soliciting her own thoughts about why he might have been so brusque – did she chat to anyone on Facebook? No. Visit Polish forums? No. What was I on about? She did not use this 'social media'. She did not dare go near it. She was terrified. Terrified. Of the men who had trafficked her. Why would she ever do anything so *mad* – so *insane* – as putting her face on the internet for all to see?

So that was me told. And told good.

I was also keen to impress upon her that we didn't believe a word of Mr Kanski's allegations, and were just anxious to put her fully in the picture about the consequences and find out if she had any thoughts herself.

'It will probably all come to nothing,' I reassured her when I'd finished. 'In fact I'm positive everything will be fine. As is John. You and I both know what happened that night, love, and Mr Kanski clearly didn't understand what was going on. Either that or he's just made a silly mistake. Or has some other axe to grind …'

Her brows came together. '*Axe* to grind?' she asked me, her expression incredulous.

'As in some other agenda. Some reason to want to get you into trouble. I know – it's insane, isn't it? I don't believe for a minute that –'

'No!' she cried, startling me by flinging her arms up in the air. 'This is wrong! *You* are wrong, Casey.' She leapt up from where we'd been sitting on the conservatory sofa. I could almost see the waves of anger coming off her. 'It is true! It's just like my friends always tell me. These people are *pigs*.' She spat the word out. 'They act so nice and friendly, and then – pfft! – they take your children away from you. They do not care for girls who have babies. They do not *like* girls who have babies. They don't care *why* it happened. That it might not be your fault. They don't *care*! It's just like I knew but had tried not to believe. It was all a plan to take my son from me! I *knew* this!'

I got up as well and tried to take hold of her, to calm her down. 'No, no, *no*, sweetheart,' I said, attempting in vain to grip her forearms. She shrugged me off. I didn't push it. 'That is *not* what is happening. I've already explained to you – this man is wrong. And we know that. We just have to wait for the evidence to come from the police so we can *prove* that he's wrong. My boss, John, and Jazz – they are both on the case here. They will make this right and you'll be able to see Ethan again soon. I promise you, Adrianna. No one is going to hold any of this against you. We all know it's nonsense, and we just have to *prove* that it's nonsense. They just have to make sure they can refute it – with the *truth*.'

'The truth?' Adrianna raged, storming off into the dining room. 'I *told* them the truth. Tyler *told* them the truth. But they don't believe it, because I am just some stupid Polish kid. I have done bad things – I know that – I wish I could change that. But they wait to pounce on me, just like my friends told me they would. And now they've done it. Tell me, Casey, when will I see my baby now, huh? Huh? I tell you. *Never*!'

This was turning out to be a nightmare, and I silently cursed my sensible husband for talking me into all this. Of course, he was right. It would have been dishonest of me to keep the truth from Adrianna and, if I was honest with myself, my reasons had probably been to avoid the exact scene we were in the middle of right now. But to do things simply for an easier life wasn't really in a foster carer's job description. Much as it irked me, we often had to take the more difficult path, for the sake of the child and their future.

I followed her into the dining room, wondering quite how many times I was going to have to say the same thing to her. 'Adrianna,' I said sternly. 'Please listen to me, properly. Listen carefully. No one – not me, not John, not Jazz, not anybody in social services – wants to take your baby away from you. Why on earth would they? It costs a fortune to have a child brought up by the state. Just from a financial point of view it would be *insane*. Emotionally, too, it is – and should be – a last resort. Yes, he could be adopted and then skip off happily into the sunset, but that's not a given, I promise you. He could end up in a bad situation, have a placement break down, have a difficult, fractured childhood – become, as a consequence, a *further* burden on the state. You understand that? You get that bit?' She grudgingly nodded.

'So, that being so, Adrianna, your friends are talking nonsense. Babies are only removed from their mothers when it's decided – *very* reluctantly – that there is no alternative. That to keep the child with the mother would be a dangerous thing to do. So *whatever* your friends have said, they are wrong, okay? If they lost their babies – or if they have been told of friends who have lost their babies – then there would have been a very good reason. That they had a drink problem, or a drugs problem, or were otherwise incapacitated – or in a violent relationship and not protecting their child from it ... Honestly, Adrianna, you are such an intelligent girl. Use your intelligence now and accept this as fact, okay?'

Again, perhaps stunned by the vociferousness of my outburst, she nodded. 'So,' I said, 'no more of this silly talk, okay? No one thinks for a moment that you have done anything wrong. But procedures must be followed – you'd want that, would you not, if the boot were on the other foot? – so, yes, we have to wait, but that is all, okay? So, patience. Because John has a job to do, and that's to deal professionally with everything. And when that silly man made that silly report about you' – how I'd have liked to use a stronger word than 'silly' – 'then his job is obviously to *approach* it professionally. As in look into it, gather evidence of its dubiousness and report back that there is no case to answer. And once that's happened – which it will – things will go back to normal, I *promise* you.'

Adrianna sighed, walked into the living room and slumped down on the sofa. 'But it is ruined now anyway,' she said. 'Your boss, John, will always have a doubt about me now, won't he? That perhaps I *was* drinking, that perhaps I *was* the cause, that maybe I *did* start trouble for Tyler and Denver.' She looked up at me, her eyes pooling with unshed tears. 'That is just human nature. You have the same saying we do in Poland? About smoke without fire?' Then she burst into tears, deep, shuddering sobs. 'Oh, Casey, I just want my baby back. I need my baby *so* bad. And every day longer, I see him slipping away. I just want a *chance*. Is that so much? Just a chance?'

I pulled her close and let her cry. 'Sweetheart,' I said, 'you don't need to ask for a chance because you have done nothing wrong. And I swear to you, Adrianna, John knows this. He is just following protocol. He *has* to follow protocol. You understand protocol? Procedure? Lots of new words today, eh?'

I felt her face change against my chest. A wan smile, I hoped.

'I know protocol,' Adrianna said. She sniffed and then looked up at me. 'And you promise me, Casey? You can promise me about Ethan again soon? I will not go out again, I swear. I will be good mother. This I swear on my life.'

Two things, I thought. One, that she would, and must, go out again. No stupid boy – or spiteful man – was going to put paid to that. Two, that, in reality, I could promise her nothing. *Should* promise her nothing, moreover. But, just on instinct, I decided to go against protocol myself. I didn't care, and I would fight this one to the end all by myself if I had to. I raised my hand solemnly. 'I swear to you, sweetheart,' I told her, 'this will all be over, very soon, and you will see Ethan again.'

Then, when she went upstairs to shower, I crossed my fingers.

Chapter 20

In the meantime, fingers crossed still, I continued to seethe. I seethed all the rest of Monday and I seethed all of Tuesday. Seethed internally, obviously, because I was a grown-up and knew how to, but every hour that passed – with the whole imbroglio still not sorted out and no contact visit on the horizon – just made me seethe all the more.

We talked it all through, Mike and I, and we were both of a mind. That we could absolutely trust Tyler and Adrianna, and that whatever was the driving force behind that cruel, destructive act was something that had nothing to do with any of us.

'We've got to look at it logically,' he said on the Wednesday evening, as we both lay in bed staring at the ceiling again. 'The way I see it, it's either one thing or the other. Either he's got some personal reason for wanting Adrianna not to have her baby back – which she is entirely unaware of – or he's got his own unrelated reasons for having a downer on teenagers generally, with a special emphasis on teenagers in care – with whom he's obviously had quite a few dealings.'

'I can't believe it's the first,' I said. 'Well, unless by some incredible coincidence he's one of the customers at whatever illegal brothel that gang of trafficking scumbags was running.'

'No, you're right,' Mike said. 'I can't see it either. We're much too far away.'

'Plus,' I added, 'he was so moody when he came to us. As in immediately moody, you know? And that was before he'd so much as clapped eyes on Adrianna. As in he didn't want to do the job at all.'

'But isn't that his job?'

'Apparently not. He was helping out, as far as I can remember. His real job is translating other stuff – written stuff – for social services. Reports. Pamphlets. Information packs and so on. You know, a desk job. Well, as far as I know.'

'So his axe to grind is more about young people generally. Which makes me think he's got' – he put his fingers in quote marks – '"issues".'

'Well, yah boo bloody sucks to him, frankly,' I fumed. '*He's* got issues? He should try losing his father, having his stepfather sexually assault him, having to run away to Britain only to find he's been brought over as a sex slave. He should try *all* of that, and see how many "issues" he ends up with. And don't get me *started* on –'

Mike placed a hand on my arm. 'I have absolutely no intention of doing so,' he said. Then, sensibly, he pinged off the light.

Since there was nothing I could personally do to help sort it all out, I did as I was told, i.e. nothing. Just kept jollying Adrianna along, promising her she would see Ethan soon, and desperately hoping I was telling her the truth. It actually wasn't that hard, because I knew Adrianna better than anyone else who was involved with her and I was supremely confident that she *would* see him again. After all, when the police provided the paperwork that would refute Mr Kanski's claims, it should be a simple formality to put the whole thing to one side. And with my more philosophical head on, I even managed to become reasonably sanguine – this was, after all, probably just the first of many injustices, irritations and plan-wrecking events that were likely to occur in Adrianna's new life. There were still so many hoops to jump through that it was insane to get in such a flap over this one.

But when a week passed, and then another, and there was still nothing doing, I began to get ants, bees *and* bugs in my own pants, and seriously considered going down to the police station myself, sneaking under the counter and doing a smash and grab raid on their evidence room.

But then the call came. And, thankfully, on a Thursday. Had John been spying on me from behind a hedge, worried I might actually do just that? Lauren and Adrianna had literally *just* driven off.

'You might want to sit down,' he said.

'Oh, no …' I groaned.

'Don't worry. It's not bad news. All good. Sanction lifted. Everything's full steam ahead again.'

My sigh of relief was so huge that all the air left my lungs. I gulped in a huge, happy in-breath. Then I sat down and listened. And John surprised me. Really surprised me.

If you put us side by side and had to choose which of us was the more generally fiery and gung-ho, you'd say me – *I'd* say me – every time. We were both professionals, but John was very much the 'professionals' professional', in that, generally speaking, he did everything by the book, which, as a senior member of the fostering agency he absolutely should.

But in this, so frustrated by the lack of forward motion, he went off piste, mixed his metaphors and stuck his neck out.

'I just couldn't stop myself,' he admitted. 'Because it was driving me nuts. So once it was clear that the wheels of justice had got stuck in a metaphorical M25 tailback, I simply picked up the phone and asked Mr Kanski what he thought he was doing myself.'

'You never,' I said, shocked. 'Isn't that harassment or something? Are you even allowed to speak to him at *all*?'

'Erm, pass,' he said.

'Go you!' I said. 'A man after my own heart! Go on, then. Shoot. What did he say?'

'Well, at first, exactly what we probably both thought he would, i.e. pretty much the same thing he'd said in his letter. After a lot of bluster of the "Why would you imagine I'd speak to you about this?" kind.'

'To which you said?'

'That I was just wondering, that was all. Wondering if he was completely sure of what he *had* seen, because it seemed so at odds with *both* the young people I knew quite well.'

'God, yes, *Tyler*. He wouldn't know Tyler's connection to you, would he?'

'Exactly. And I think it floored him a bit.'

'Good. And?'

'And I told him that I also wondered why he was so sure Adrianna had done the things he'd said, given that the police had seen the incident rather differently.'

'And?'

'And that was it.'

'What was it?'

'That was the key thing. That was really why I couldn't stop myself from calling him. I mentioned the *police*. That's *why* I called him, Casey. Because it had suddenly hit me that he couldn't possibly know about the police being involved. I worked it out. He'd made no mention of it in his letter – and you'd expect that, wouldn't you? If he had known they were there? Surely? That he'd either say something like 'the police had to be called' or have even called them himself. But he did neither. And then I looked at the date – and he had written his letter about Adrianna the next day. And I didn't get your log report about the incident till I picked up your email on the Monday morning, and it didn't make it into the file till the Tuesday.'

I was trying to keep up. 'But that still doesn't explain the disparity, or why he did it.'

'Patience. I'm coming to that now. So, as soon as he heard about the police coming he went quiet, so of course I said, "Oh, weren't you there when the police arrived, then?" And he blustered again a bit – you know, "I didn't need to be. I'd already seen enough" and so on – at which point I told him that the police had taken statements from everyone involved and that they had, in fact, charged the *other* boy with assault. I also told him the other boy was already known to the police and that nobody had been under the influence of alcohol. At which point he began back-tracking, *big* time. Specially when I told him the police correspondence on the matter was in the post – and that it would effectively put the lie to his mad, trumped-up version of events. Well, I didn't say that last bit, obviously. Not in those exact words. But I'm sure he got the gist. As he should. Because, in reality, he could even be sued for libel, couldn't he?'

'So what's he going to do now?' I asked. 'Write another letter, explaining that he got it all wrong?'

'Pretty much. Though it's a moot point now anyway. The statements have already arrived, so it's just a question of filing paperwork and putting it to bed really.'

Which was obviously a relief, but I still didn't get it. 'But why did he do it in the *first* place? That still doesn't figure. What possessed him? What did she ever do to him?'

'Okay,' said John. 'So this bit's strictly between you and me. I did some digging,' he said. I smiled to myself. That was us two – always digging. 'And though it's all hearsay, it does make some sense of it.'

'*What* does?' I said, exasperated. He was enjoying this far too much.

'So here's what I've heard, in a nutshell. Married man. Two kids. Working as a translator for the service. Though not the desk job – out in the field, then. On call. Home visit stuff. Interviews. Mostly dealing with immigrants who have little or no English, and so on. And he gets involved with a girl – this was a good half dozen years ago. A young Polish girl who he's been working with regularly. Has some sort of midlife crisis, and has an affair. The girl gets pregnant. Puts pressure on. The wife chucks him out. Takes the kids. Moves away. End of marriage. Then the girl leaves him too. *Et voilà*. One deeply, deeply unhappy divorcee. Can't cope. Changes area. Moves to desk job.'

'Oh, my word …' I said, shocked. 'So Mike was spot on. He said it would be personal. He said he'd have issues. And you know what? I saw something on Facebook just the other day. Let me think how it went. Something like, "When somebody is cruel to you, remember that it's nothing to do with you and a reflection on them. No normal person tries to destroy someone else's life." That's the gist, anyway. Blimey.'

'It's more than that, Casey, in all seriousness. He's only just back after a long period off sick with stress. Not just issues, I'd say. Major mental health issues. And, of course, *now* it comes to light – now it's chugged up the line a bit – that this letter isn't an isolated incident.'

'So he's a serial letter writer, then. A serial "offender". And our poor Adrianna just happened to be in the firing line. Jeepers.'

John sighed, as if, depressingly, it had all worked out as expected. 'So I suppose we should feel sorry for him, shouldn't we?'

'You know what? I think I do, John. In a weird sort of way. He's obviously ill.'

'And there but for the grace of God, eh? That's what I can't help thinking. Anyway, it's over.'

I *did* feel a bit sorry for Mr Kanski, now I knew more. It must be no joke to have so much bitterness lodged in your heart that it spills so corrosively into your head. But it being over at least meant it could begin again.

After all the upset – and, no, I never spoke a word of my new intelligence to Adrianna – it felt a little like finally breathing out. And, sure enough, two days later Jazz called with the news that we could travel back down to London to see Ethan the following week.

And it had clearly been a shrewd move to get Adrianna working, because she put the couple of weeks' worth of pocket money to very good use, and was able to arrive at the house bearing presents. She'd bought Ethan a teddy bear, and a beautiful little striped sailor outfit, which the foster mum, Sarah, made a quite delightful fuss over, commenting on how amazing Adrianna was for getting the size absolutely perfect, as if being able to do so was some divine maternal gift few were lucky enough to have

253

been bestowed with, and generally making Adrianna feel wonderful.

'And he knew me. I am sure of it,' she enthused on the way home. 'Did you see the way he smiled? Casey, you were right – he didn't forget me.'

'You see?' I said. 'A baby knows. That's the thing. A baby knows its mother.'

'And I must buy a mobile phone next time I get paid. Just a cheap one, to take photos of Ethan,' she added. She then sighed deeply. 'Oh, Casey, I wish they lived nearer to us. I hate to leave him. My heart hurts *so* much.'

I really didn't think she could have put it any better.

I hadn't told Adrianna, and wouldn't be doing so, but the day before the visit I'd made a decision of my own while Adrianna was with my sister. Having chewed it over with Mike, I'd driven down to see John in his office and run a plan by him – that in the short term Ethan should simply come to us. '*Only* in the short term,' I emphasised, 'because I do see it as short term. She'll be 17 soon, and once she's acclimatised to motherhood it should be no problem to move her on to supported lodgings.'

I also mentioned that, should she want it, Adrianna could work more hours in Truly Scrumptious, which would help her save up for the necessary expenses that lay ahead.

But John wouldn't budge – not even an inch – on his resounding 'no'.

He also raised a hand, all the better to tick his reasons off on it, and this was before he'd even offered me a coffee.

'If Adrianna wants her baby back,' he'd said, 'then she has to be assessed properly. Which means the assessment has to take place in a neutral setting. And before you jump down my throat, I *know* you've had a mother and baby placement in the past, and –'

'Exactly,' I squeaked. He ignored me. 'What happened with Emma was different, Casey. You *know* that. She came to you pregnant. The circumstances here are *totally* different and, in order to fairly assess this as viable, we need to be able to see how Adrianna copes, on her *own*, with these gradual introductions to her baby's life.'

'Okay, I *accept* it,' I said sulkily. 'But I still don't understand it. It would make things so much simpler if she just stayed with us.'

'Ethan is four months old now,' John continued gently. 'He has routines and is used to his life as it is, simple as that may be. So it's for Adrianna to show that she can fit in with *him*, which she won't be able to do with you hovering in the background and her life continuing very much as before.'

'I don't hover,' I said indignantly.

'Casey, you *do*,' he said firmly. 'And how will you stop yourself? No way can she make the transition she needs to while billeted at the Watson Boutique Hotel. Seriously, there is a reason for everything we do, and this is one such – she needs to do this bit on her own. But what I *can* tell you is that we are actively looking for a placement a lot nearer to you. A temporary set of carers who are trained to do this very job. They keep babies in their home solely for these kinds of assessment purposes.'

'Really?' I asked, surprised. I hadn't realised such special-ist foster carers even existed. But then I didn't know every-thing about everything, clearly. Because it seemed they did.

'Really,' John assured me. And he graciously didn't rub my nose in it. 'And we even think we might have found the very people for the job.'

Now my ears pricked up. This was more like it.

For the next couple of weeks I didn't have time to wonder what might be happening in the background because I was obliged to start thinking about what I'd been sidelined from thinking about; namely that there were three birth-days coming up. Not to mention Easter, which was late this year, which meant I might as well lump everything together: Jackson's eighth, Marley Mae's third and, of course, Adrianna's seventeenth, all kind of sprinkled with an Easter-ish theme.

It seemed the only sensible option was to hold one massive joint party. And as constant checks online seemed to confirm that the weather was being kind for a change, I decided to make it a garden party too.

Which was not big stress – should the heavens open, we'd simply decamp inside again, and either way I'd benefit because a triple party meant only one manic bout of clean-ing, and since Mike, Kieron and Riley's David turned into master chefs at the very mention of the word 'barbecue', I wouldn't have much cooking to do either.

In fact, I thought, pleased with myself for such excellent forward thinking, it would be a perfect opportunity to further Adrianna's domestic education. I had a long list of items she had to start becoming proficient at, and two perfect birthday cakes, one for Jackson and one for Marley Mae, seemed as good a place as any to start.

'How's she doing anyway?' Riley asked, nodding into the garden at Adrianna on the morning of the big day. We were all busy doing our own final preparations before anyone else arrived, and Adrianna was outside with Mike, unwrapping burgers and sausages. She glanced up and, spotting us, waved.

I waved back, feeling excited at the prospect of her seeing the surprise birthday cake I'd organised for her. Not made for her. My domestic skills didn't quite run to Premier League party-cake-baking, and since I imagined she'd not had a birthday cake in years, I'd had Riley – who was *the* party-cake supremo bar none – concoct a huge spiral of lavishly decorated cupcakes, their toppings a riot of eye-popping spring flowers.

'Fine,' I said to my clever daughter, who'd just stashed the surprise away for later. 'In fact better than fine. She's coping really well, considering. *Amazingly* well.'

I continued to watch Adrianna, realising how different she had always seemed from the kids we usually fostered – and from day one. 'This has been one weird placement,' I mused, as I continued to watch her through the conservatory window.

Riley looked at me quizzically. 'Weird? How d'you mean, Mum?' she asked.

I thought for a moment. 'Just the complete absence of all the things we usually have to deal with, I suppose. No meltdowns, no door-slamming. No behavioural issues. No dashing to the phone to call the emergency duty team in the small hours. No violence. No self-harming ...' I smiled as I trailed off. The list of troubles she *didn't* display was probably endless. 'Honestly, in some ways it's been more like having an international student come to stay with us. You know? Or an *au pair* even. Or a lodger.' I looked at my daughter. 'Do you think they breed them tougher in Poland? Is that it? Because one thing is for sure. She's been so little trouble – you know, on a day-to-day level – that it's all too easy to forget what she's been through. You'd think she'd ... I don't know ...' I faltered. 'It's hard to explain, but, you know, where has it all *gone*? All that psychological trauma. All the fear and the loneliness and the sense of betrayal. All the horror of everything that's happened to her. You know, since she told me her real story that day at the hospital, she's barely mentioned any of it again. I mean, yes, she's made the odd comment – about her dad, about the friends she made. But that's *it*. So where's it *gone*? It's like she's – I don't know – wiped the disk in her brain. Isn't the human psyche strange?'

'You're telling me,' Riley said. She considered it for a moment. 'But maybe that's the best way of dealing with it all. For *her*. You know, I appreciate we do all this training about psychology and all that, and I get that. And if a child has major issues because of something they're not dealing with, then obviously it's important that they get help. But don't you think that, sometimes, it's better if you *can* forget? Just, you know, park it. Move on. Not keep trying to go back. It's not like she can change anything, is it?'

'She still has a mother out there somewhere. Well, if she can be called that, quite frankly.' I sighed. 'No, I shouldn't say that. I don't know her story, do I?'

'So maybe at some point in the future there will be a reconciliation there. Does funny things to you, being a mother, doesn't it? You get a whole new perspective. Perhaps she'll find a way ...'

'Nice to think so. Though right now she seems pretty set on what she wants. Which is not to go back, ever. Just to get her baby back ...'

'And that's going to keep her pretty busy. Hard business bringing up a baby as a single mum, for anyone.'

I nodded. It was another mountain yet to climb, definitely – both practically and emotionally. But she was just so fired up to get going. To reclaim the motherhood she'd almost lost. 'I just wish things could be speeded up for her,' I said. 'That she could get *on* with it. Poor thing is pining for that baby boy, and there's nothing I can do to help her.'

'But you *are* helping, Mum,' Riley said. 'Of *course* you are. Imagine if she didn't have you and Dad in her corner. Think about it. Fate has played a massive part here. If she didn't live with you two, she'd never have met Lauren, she'd never have gone to dance class, she'd probably never have gone to hospital ... or if she had, who's to say she'd have dared open up about what had happened to her? She might well have been too scared, mightn't she? She could have been carrying that pain around for years yet. No baby. End of. *For ever*. Now that, I'd say, really *would* mess with her psyche. Instead, she's in contact with her baby and in all likelihood she will get him back.'

'I just wish the whole process didn't take so *long*, though.'

Riley rolled her eyes. 'Honestly, Mum, things can't always happen at your command, you know. You just have to be a bit more patient!'

'Oh, I know,' I said, gazing out at the happy little tableau in the garden. 'But you know what I'm like. When I uncover a mystery – well, okay, in this case, sort of – I just want all the loose ends tied up as quickly as possible. I hate this feeling of being in limbo – of not knowing what's going to happen next.'

'Oh, Mother,' Riley said, shaking both her head and the salad tongs. 'You already know *exactly* what happens next. Adrianna continues to be assessed, social services decide if she's a fit mother, they help her find a flat and off she goes – simples! And listen –' We both did. 'Kieron's just put on your Blondie CD, so come on, get your groove on and have a dance, woman!'

So I did dance, and allowed myself to 'go with the flow'. Which wasn't difficult, seeing as I had all my family around me. All the kids and grandkids, Donna and Chloe, my mum and dad – even Denver, for whom I would always have a soft spot – and all of whom kindly brought gifts for all three of our birthday guests.

And, best of all, one very special gift indeed. Soppy to be so sentimental, I know, but perhaps that's just part and parcel of getting older. You've seen so much, been through stuff, learned what matters and what doesn't, and, for the first but definitely not the last time that day, I found myself feeling silly for being reduced to floods of tears.

It was just so unexpected. One minute I was standing chatting to Lauren, little Dee Dee on my hip, and the next I had Marley Mae tugging at my top and asking me to go with her to give Adrianna a special present.

So off we all toddled, whereupon I was astonished to watch my grandaughter climb onto Adrianna's knee and present her with her oh-so-precious rabbit.

'For baby Ethan,' she said. I think I actually gaped. This wasn't just any rabbit, this was the cuddly-toy-that-must-never-be-mislaid. The one she'd clung to since babyhood – her chosen 'transitional comfort item', to use the parlance. The ball of fluff that had been through the wash-dryer cycle a zillion times, the thing she simply could not be without.

Correction. I did gape. I twisted my head and gaped at Riley. But she just gave me a 'well, if that's what she wants to do' kind of shrug.

'It's a wabbit,' Marley Mae went on. Adrianna was gaping too. 'An' he was mine when I was little. But I'm a big girl today, so I don't need him no more. It's okay,' she said, presumably seeing Adrianna's doubtful expression. 'You have it for the baby. Go on – kiss him!'

'I don't know what to say,' Adrianna answered, dutifully kissing both 'wabbit' and Marley Mae. And, conscious that a change of mind might occur once my grandaughter got tired, I had to bite my lip to stop the words 'Are you sure?' coming from them. Perhaps I was underestimating her anyway.

'Thank you, my princess,' Adrianna said, her voice wobbly. 'And soon you will meet baby Ethan yourself. And I promise I will tell him that it was you that gave him his very first Easter bunny.'

And there were, it seemed, other Easter traditions for us to partake in, of a kind that went down extremely well in some quarters. With the day proving so kind, we did the triple cake candle blowing-out ceremony in the garden, and it was just after that when I caught the tail-end of a conversation that had Tyler in something of an excited spin.

'You look like you're cooking something up,' I said to the giggling teenage gaggle – teenage *and*, I noted, including Levi and Kieron.

'Tell Mum,' Tyler enthused. 'We just have to do it, don't we?' He nudged Kieron. 'It's not like we haven't got the kit for it or anything, is it?'

'I'm definitely up for it,' Kieron agreed.

'Go on then,' I said, knowing intuitively that it was going to be something I probably wouldn't approve of but would end up sanctioning anyway.

'We have this tradition in Poland,' Adrianna explained. 'It's called Wet Monday –'

'Uh-ho,' I said.

'Really, it is the best fun of all of Easter. It is the day when all the boys get water – they fill buckets, and use water pistols, and blasters –'

'And we have blasters,' said Tyler, grinning at Denver.

'And they chase the girls around. All over town, this is – *everyone* does this. And everyone gets very, very wet. It's so fun,' she finished, beaming.

My immediate thought was – *in Gdansk, on the Baltic? It would be – well, Baltic!* And my second was that there was no getting away from it. It might be Sunday, but there was no splitting hairs to be done here. Wet Monday, Polish style, was what it was going to be. I knew those gleams – in Kieron, in Tyler and, increasingly, in Levi. It would take a better woman than I was to manage to stop them.

Even had I wanted to, which I didn't. And Adrianna had been right. It was indeed 'so fun'. For everyone.

And, yes, everyone got very, *very* wet.

I would never have imagined that the day could have gone any better, but it seemed it was about to. We were just at the mopping-up stage, everyone full of birthday cake and giggles, when my mobile phone started to vibrate on the bench beside me. I glanced down at the number and grimaced. Why on earth would John Fulshaw be calling me on a Sunday afternoon? Certainly not to pass the time of day. I hoped it wasn't more bad news, but I dodged into the conservatory to take it just in case.

'Hi, Casey,' he said, 'I'm sorry to interrupt the festivities and I know you'll be busy but I wanted you to know as soon as I did. I've just taken the call.'

'What call?' I asked, cupping a hand round my other ear to drown out the noise coming from the garden. 'Is there something wrong?'

'Just the opposite,' he said brightly. 'I am the bearer of good news for a change. The assessment carers I mentioned have agreed to take Ethan. All being well, he moves in with them next week.'

'Oh, that's *brilliant*,' I said, doing a little Tyler fist-pump. I couldn't wait to see the expression on Adrianna's face.

'Oh, but there's more. Something that I think will make your day as well. Casey, they only live two minutes away from your house.'

This was stunning news. Almost unbelievable, in fact. '*What*? Really? Oh my God, John! So close! What are the chances?'

'Slim to zero, I'd say. But sometimes the sun shines on the righteous, I guess. So yes, really. Almost neighbours.'

'So do I know them?'

'I don't think so,' he said. 'They're fairly new to the area. Probably heard on the grapevine what a nice class of people live roundabouts. But, no, they say they don't know you, so I'm assuming not – except perhaps by sight. Which might be the case because they're practically round the corner from you.'

This was marvellous news. For both us and Adrianna. 'Oh,' I said, joyfully, 'I *cannot* wait to tell her!'

'Listen, about that. D'you think you could put her on the phone? Call me soft, but I'd really like to tell her this myself. I feel I'm always the bearer of bad tidings, so it would be nice to be the one giving her some good news for a change.'

'Oh, of course!' I said. Bless him. And he made a good point. All the hard work he did behind the scenes, making a difference – did it really get the appreciation it deserved? Probably not. I told him to hang on and dashed out into the garden, phone in hand, dragging Adrianna back with me to somewhere she could properly hear.

'It's for you,' I said, grinning as I handed her my mobile. Then stood and waited as she listened and the smile began to creep up her face. 'Oh,' she said, finally, 'dzieki, *dzieki*!' Then a bunch of stuff in Polish that I didn't understand.

'I'm so sorry,' she said, once she'd managed to regain some composure. 'I was so excited I forgot to speak in English. Forgive me.'

As if she needed to apologise. 'Don't be daft,' I said. 'I just wondered what you said to John, that was all.'

She blushed. She was a beautiful girl. Inside and out. 'Oh, just that he is now my *ziom*, like Tyler. And that this is the best birthday present I could wish for.' Then she put a hand to her mouth, clearly having second thoughts. 'Oh, but I hope I was not too familiar!'

No danger of that, I thought. Bless her. I could already imagine the width of John's grin.

Chapter 21

Because I simply couldn't resist it, I got the assessment carers' address and phone number from John, and the following Tuesday, with his blessing, Adrianna and I set off round there to say hello – and it really was just a hop and a skip away.

They were another youngish couple, not so different from Jack and Sarah down in London, but with one major difference: they had no children of their own. Which intrigued me – I knew foster carers were like Heinz beans, and came in 57 varieties, but this was one variety I'd not come across before.

Which seemed logical, I mused, as we crossed the small park that separated our respective streets. A first baby is such a massive upheaval in anyone's life that I couldn't quite get my head round how they coped with what they did without being parents themselves. But then I mused a little longer and saw the ridiculousness of my reasoning. The world was stuffed full of midwives who'd never given birth themselves, wasn't it? Not to mention child psychologists, and paediatricians, and nursery nurses. There was such a thing as training, wasn't there? Really, why not this as well?

We headed out of the other side of the park, Adrianna in raptures about all of it. I'd pointed out the play park and the place where the path ran down to the woods. 'There's a stream down there, too,' I said. 'Perfect for pond dipping.'

She almost clapped her hands in glee at this and at first I wondered why so much excitement. After all, she must have seen plenty of parks before. Not to mention slept in a few from time to time. But then it struck me. She was already making that transition. To seeing the world and all that was in it through her child's eyes.

The woman, Alex, was as nice in person as she'd seemed on the phone, ushering us smilingly into a sunny back room that overlooked the woods, and which smelt pleasingly – certainly to my nostrils – of coffee and furniture polish.

'This couldn't be better, could it?' she enthused. 'I couldn't believe it when John told me we were so close. It will make the transition so much easier, won't it? How are you doing, Adrianna? So nice to meet you. I'll bet you are counting the days.'

'And the hours, and the minutes …' I added, laughing.

'And the seconds, too,' Adrianna confirmed. 'I hope it's not so much longer to wait.'

Alex reassured her that she didn't think it would be. 'And as soon as he is here, we'll all sit down and make a plan.'

And it would be a plan that would very much include me. I was well aware that once Ethan was transferred into Alex and her partner's care my own role in respect to Adrianna would also change. To some extent, I'd no longer be just a bringer of love and security. I would also become an assessor of her as well; it would be our joint reporting on how she was coping with the demands of motherhood, not to mention whether she was making strides towards independence, that would make up much of the material that would decide the outcome for them both.

And I had a good feeling about the couple from the outset. I hadn't known what to expect, but my thoughts had certainly drifted. There's a type of childcare guru, usually childless, that tends to polarise opinion, due to the uncompromising nature of their methods. All lickety-spit, no-nonsense, 'spare the rod and spoil the child' edicts – but Alex wasn't like that at all. I asked her how she'd come to do such a specialist kind of fostering.

'I'm not sure,' she said. 'I just saw an advert and it appealed to me. I've been around babies all my life, as has Simon – we both grew up in very large families. And it just kind of spoke to me.' She grinned at Adrianna. 'So here I am.'

She said they'd been doing it for two years now – exactly what they'd be doing with Ethan and Adrianna – and that they were in no rush to have children of their own just yet. 'I think we'll know when the time is right,' she finished. 'Or, more accurately, the bank account will, anyway. Though my mum disagrees.' She smiled indulgently. 'Bless her. She's convinced it'll put us off and that she'll never be a grandma. But quite the contrary.'

I nodded. 'I know what you mean. I thought our fostering might put my daughter off having children too. But she has three of them, and she also does some fostering herself. Only respite, for the moment, at least till the little ones are a bit older. Still, I'd never have thought she'd choose to do that. Perhaps it's just a job that chooses *you*.'

'And how about you, honey?' Alex said, turning to Adrianna. 'Have you any idea what you want to do with the rest of your life yet?'

It took me slightly aback, and in a wholly positive way. I felt almost chastened. We were all so focused on the traumas of the present that I don't think we'd really thought to look beyond them. I loved Alex for that – that she saw something beyond the girl in care, in terrible straits, whose circumstances had led her to let go of her baby and who would now have to spend a difficult, scrutinised, complicated few months – if not more – trying to get him back again. I decided I liked Alex very much.

Adrianna took the question seriously, as was her way. 'I think I would like to be a teacher. Maybe music. I played piano as a child. Which I liked very much. And the ballet.' She smiled shyly. 'But perhaps that is a little *too* ambitious.'

Alex shook her head. 'Not at all,' she said. 'It's good to have ambition.'

'But for now my ambition is to be a good mother to Ethan. And now he will be close ...' She glanced at me. 'I will be able to see him more?'

Alex beamed at her. 'Of course you will. In fact, that's *exactly* what you'll do. Part of our job – mine and Simon's – is to take a step back while Ethan is staying here, and let you do most of the caring. Which means that, hopefully, after your first couple of visits, you will be feeding him, bathing him, taking him for walks and, most glamorous of all, changing his dirty nappies. How does that sound?'

Adrianna looked dumbstruck, her jaw hanging open. 'Oh!' she said. 'I really get to do all of those things? That's so great.'

Alex laughed. 'Of course you do, silly! He's your baby, not mine. He's just staying with us for a little while. I'm here to guide you and help you if you need it, of course, but mainly I just have to let you prove that you can meet his needs. That means showing that you can look after him properly. I have to write reports, of course, so that everybody who matters knows how well you are doing, but really that's about it.'

It seemed a good opportunity to add my two-pence worth. 'And I have to do the same,' I reminded her. 'Now that your status has changed, and you will be preparing to move on, I also have to write reports, as John probably told you. To prove that you can look after yourself as well.'

'Independent Polish girl,' Adrianna said, smiling happily. 'John explained that. I have to be able to save money, to cook and clean, to wash my clothes. Which I do.'

'Which you have *always* done,' I agreed, grinning at her. 'Your speciality!'

* * *

Before we left, Alex pulled me to one side while Adrianna had nipped to use the toilet. 'You know, Casey,' she said, 'we really don't mind her calling daily, if that works for you. Or at least every evening to tuck him in. She must be hurting so badly, and forming that bond is so important, don't you think?'

I could have kissed Alex. What a lovely, understanding young woman she was. And she was spot on. For all that I'd tried to reassure Adrianna to the contrary, it had been nagging away at me for a while now that Ethan *would* be forming attachments with other maternal figures, and that Adrianna would miss out on such an important part of the bonding process.

'I can read stories to him at bedtime,' she enthused to Tyler that evening over tea. 'And sing him lullabies. Polish lullabies, like my father sang to me. I can't wait.'

Tyler pulled a face. 'I'd stick to the bedtime stories if I were you,' he joked. 'I've heard your singing voice, and you're no Mariah Carey.'

'You cheeky thing,' she replied, giving him a friendly punch. 'You'd better shape up if you want me to let you be his Uncle Tyler. You need to be like Casey says. In my good book.'

'Books,' Tyler said, needing to get the last word in. 'You mean books, as in plural.'

Adrianna tutted. 'Yeah, like, Tyler, what*eva*,' she drawled. I smiled. Her linguistic education was obviously ongoing.

As was her education on all fronts, with special emphasis on home economics and PSE. And, from now on, all carefully documented by me. Over the next few days I began compiling the report that would be submitted to Panel, who would sit and deliberate once this period of assessment was deemed complete. I had to detail how Adrianna would cope with day-to-day life unsupported, from whether she could cook decent and balanced meals for herself and, obviously, her baby, to whether she knew how to operate all the household appliances. She needed to be proficient at washing and ironing, and to demonstrate that she could prioritise effectively. And she had to understand and manage a budget.

This was all standard stuff, really, for any girl or boy at her age who was in the process of moving on from a foster family. But it was crucially important for Adrianna. It would mean the difference between going on to a mother-and-baby placement – another specialised form of fostering, with its own rules and protocols – or straight into a flat of her own, with a support package in place.

I also encouraged her to think about her plans for the future. In the longer term, yes, she should aspire to be whatever she wanted, but, just as was the case for any teenage single mum coming from the care system, the immediate future would involve many constraints. She needed to decide whether she would take a job and find some childcare, or go to college and make use of their crèche. All of which meant navigating the complexities of the benefit system and, given how long it would probably take even for her to get a National Insurance number, I thought that this might prove a problem. John, however, reassured me that

I shouldn't worry on that score. Jasmine was a whizz, he said, and, if that was Adrianna's choice, she would be able to guide her through the paperwork.

Adrianna was single-minded, however. 'I am an independent Polish girl,' she reminded me. It had almost become her mantra. 'So I will work. I must work. It is only fair.'

Which put me in mind, once again, of the ladies who'd been so rude about her in Truly Scrumptious. Oh, what I would have given to have had them hear her.

But Adrianna's immediate future was a great deal less complex. And set to begin the following Tuesday, when my mobile began chirruping, heralding the news she'd waited so long to hear.

I handed the phone to her, so Alex could inform her herself. 'He is here! My baby's here!' she sang. 'They have delivered him. It is like Christmas!'

And despite the warmth of the spring sunshine and the leaves beginning to unfurl on the trees, it did feel a bit like that, as well.

Fostering brings with it all shades of emotion. Peaks and troughs, high and lows, whatever you want to call them – that hackneyed phrase 'it's a rollercoaster ride' is hackneyed for a reason because, more often than not, it's so apt. Because there is rarely, if ever, an even keel with a looked-after child. Every one is different; is differently damaged and so has their own unique needs. Each requires different approaches, different goals and different handling, and the desired outcomes, be they ambitious or necessarily modest, are never guaranteed.

There were no guarantees with Adrianna. Only a fool would blithely assume that it would all work out fine. She was 17, far from home and had the world on her shoulders. She had a whole world of struggles ahead of her right now. But as I watched her push her new pram – which was, of financial necessity, an old pram – along the route that would be her regular walk for several months to come now, I decided that, just for once, I would indulge myself. Let myself believe that, in this case, it *would* all be fine. That our independent Polish girl would live up to the label she had given herself; test her mettle, prove her worth, make a good life for her child. And yah boo sucks to all the doubters, as Tyler might say.

'Casey,' Adrianna said, interrupting my reverie. 'You are *crying*! Look! All the tears that are rolling down your face!'

I stopped on the path and touched my cheek. Looked down at the baby, who was sleeping. Turned and looked at Adrianna. Then smiled. And then tutted. 'Well, *you're* a fine one to talk, I must say!'

Then, side by side, crying, we carried on our way.

Epilogue

Although Adrianna wasn't with us for a long time, she had a huge impact in our lives. The inner strength and resilience she displayed not only humbled us but also taught us that not all chaotic beginnings result in fractured lives. This was a big learning experience for us and enabled us to sometimes look beyond that which we thought must be broken, and search instead for the thread of hope and the yearning for something better. Because despite what I had always thought – that trauma will always have a profound adverse effect on a child – Adrianna showed us that this wasn't always the case. She helped us realise that some children are able to set their past to one side, no matter how horrific, and take what is good in their lives and move forward.

Adrianna was contacted by the police shortly after being reunited with her baby, and she was able to identify a couple of the 'mug shots' she was presented with. Recognising faces, however, was not the same as providing names, and the last we heard was they had not come back to her again. And she was happy about that. She really did want to put the past behind her. Her *whole* past. Her life, she was determined, would start afresh.

She worked hard for four months to prove that she loved and could take care of her baby boy, and then, very unexpectedly, the assessment carers, Alex and Simon, offered her a place in their home for another month. This enabled her to care for Ethan full time, so that she'd get a clear picture of what the future was going to be like. They were – and are – such amazing people. Adrianna naturally jumped at this generous opportunity and it was the best thing she could have done – although, obviously, despite her still being so close by, we all missed her presence in the house terribly.

Of course, we saw her often, because she visited regularly with Ethan Jakob (as he is now called), which allowed us to feel we were a part of his life. And, after that, Adrianna was offered a flat of her own, and a moving-on care worker who would support her for as long as she needed it.

She did also make it to college. Though continuing to work, she enrolled on a college course in design and also, via the persuasive powers of the lovely Jazz, got social services to pay for private piano lessons out of their care-leavers' budget. And quite rightly, in my book, which was why they were happy to; it would be another string to her bow (or, more accurately, piano), giving her further employment options in the future. Will she eventually become a teacher? I certainly wouldn't bet against it.

We all still keep in touch with Adrianna – her birthday buddy Marley Mae very much included – and Tyler – her *ziom* – even goes to stay over from time to time. She is still single at the moment and doing very well for herself, and Ethan Jakob, two and a half now, is like any other toddler; sometimes a 'little angel' and other times a 'little tyke', switching between both several times on any given day. Needless to say, with Tyler's continuing input, she now speaks English like a native.

The investigations into the trafficking of 'hidden children' continue.

TOPICS FOR READING-GROUP DISCUSSION

1. Having learned about 'hidden children', do you think that when these children are discovered they should be sent back to their own countries? Bear in mind that British courts possess the right to take jurisdiction themselves or to pass the case on to the country concerned.

2. When British courts take a given case they use various methods or 'tests' to establish whether a child from another European country should be allowed to remain. One of these is called 'habitual residence', which looks at how the child is integrated into our country and the consequences of uprooting them. Another is called 'best interests'. What do you think the courts mean by this, and, if Adrianna had been looked at, what do you imagine her check list of best interests would have looked like?

3. Although human trafficking is often a hidden crime and accurate statistics are difficult to obtain, researchers estimate that more than 80 per cent of trafficking victims are female. Over 50 per cent of human trafficking victims are children. What do you think may have happened to Adrianna if she hadn't escaped when she did? Consider her pregnancy in particular.

4. Although it is estimated that 30 per cent of humans trafficked are sold into the sex industry, discuss the other areas in which vulnerable men, women and children are useful to traffickers.

5. Since the advent of free movement within most of Europe, discuss the implications you think this has had on our resources as a country. Given the unknown figures – which are thought to be immense – how do you think we could address this? Do you even think we *should* address this? Do we have a moral responsibility to the children of the wider world?

6. What about the children like Adrianna? She tells Casey she hasn't been honest about her baby as she is frightened she 'will be taken to a detention centre', in other words become a virtual prisoner. Do you think we should have a dedicated 'safe haven' for these girls to run to? A place where they could get help without judgement? What would this resource look like?

CASEY WATSON

One woman determined to
make a difference.

Read Casey's poignant
memoirs and be inspired.

Five-year-old Justin was desperate and helpless

Six years after being taken into care, Justin has had 20 failed placements. Casey and her family are his last hope.

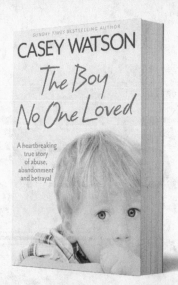

THE BOY NO ONE LOVED

A damaged girl haunted by her past

Sophia pushes Casey to the limits, threatening the safety of the whole family. Can Casey make a difference in time?

CRYING FOR HELP

Abused siblings who do not know what it means to be loved

With new-found security and trust, Casey helps Ashton and Olivia to rebuild their lives.

LITTLE PRISONERS

Branded 'vicious and evil', eight-year-old Spencer asks to be taken into care

Casey and her family are disgusted: kids aren't born evil. Despite the challenges Spencer brings, they are determined to help him find a loving home.

TOO HURT TO STAY

A young girl secretly caring for her mother

Abigail has been dealing with pressures no child should face. Casey has the difficult challenge of helping her to learn to let go.

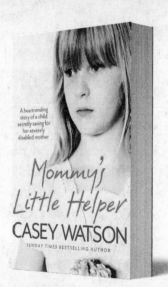

MOMMY'S LITTLE HELPER

Two boys with an unlikely bond

With Georgie and Jenson, Casey is facing her toughest test yet.

BREAKING THE SILENCE

A teenage mother
and baby in need of
a loving home

At fourteen, Emma is just
a child herself – and one
who's never been properly
mothered.

Eleven-year-old Tyler
has stabbed his
stepmother and has
nowhere to go

With his birth mother
dead and a father
who doesn't want him,
what can be done to stop
his young life spiralling
out of control?

What is the secret behind Imogen's silence?

Discover the shocking and devastating past of a child with severe behavioural problems.

THE GIRL WITHOUT A VOICE

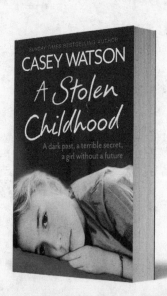

Kiara appears tired and distressed, and the school wants Casey to take her under her wing for a while

On the surface, everything points to a child who is upset that her parents have separated. The horrific truth, however, shocks Casey to the core.

A STOLEN CHILDHOOD

Flip is being raised by her alcoholic mother, and comes to Casey after a fire at their home

Flip has Foetal Alcohol Syndrome (FAS), but it soon turns out that this is just the tip of the iceberg . . .

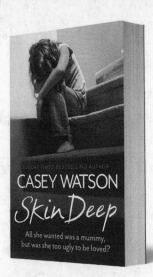

SKIN DEEP

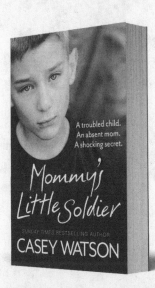

Leo isn't a bad lad, but his frequent absences from school mean he's on the brink of permanent exclusion

Leo is clearly hiding something, and Casey knows that if he is to have any kind of future, it's up to her to find out the truth.

MOMMY'S LITTLE SOLDIER

Adrianna arrives on Casey's doorstep with no possessions, no English and no explanation

It will be a few weeks before Casey starts getting the shocking answers to her questions . . .

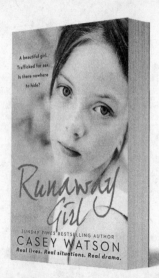

RUNAWAY GIRL

Bella's father is on a ventilator, fighting for his life, while her mother is currently on remand in prison, charged with his attempted murder.

Bella is the only witness.

THE SILENT WITNESS

AVAILABLE AS E-BOOK ONLY

Cameron is a sweet boy who seems happy in his skin – making him rather different from most of the other children Casey has cared for

But what happens when Cameron disappears? Will Casey's worst fears be realised?

CASEY WATSON
SUNDAY TIMES BESTSELLING AUTHOR
Just a Boy

An inspiring and heartwarming short story

JUST A BOY

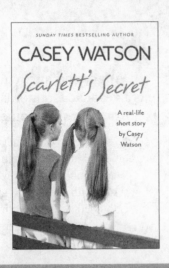

SUNDAY *TIMES* BESTSELLING AUTHOR
CASEY WATSON
Scarlett's Secret

A real-life short story by Casey Watson

Jade and Scarlett, seventeen-year-old twins, share a terrible secret

Can Casey help them come to terms with the truth and rediscover their sibling connection?

SCARLETT'S SECRET

AVAILABLE AS E-BOOK ONLY

Nathan has a sometime alter ego called Jenny who is the only one who knows the secrets of his disturbed past

But where is Jenny when she is most needed?

NO PLACE FOR NATHAN

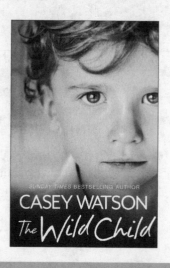

Angry and hurting, eight-year-old Connor is from a broken home

As streetwise as they come, he's determined to cause trouble. But Casey is convinced there is a frightened child beneath the swagger.

THE WILD CHILD

Six-year-old Darby is naturally distressed at being removed from her parents just before Christmas

And when the shocking and sickening reason is revealed, a Happy New Year seems an impossible dream as well . . .

THE LITTLE PRINCESS

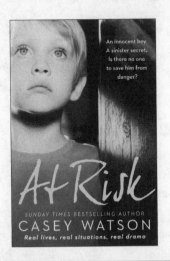

Adam is brought to Casey while his mum recovers in hospital – just for a few days

But a chance discovery reveals that Casey has stumbled upon something altogether more sinister . . .

AT RISK

FEEL HEART.
FEEL HOPE.
READ CASEY.

Discover more about Casey Watson.
Visit www.caseywatson.co.uk